AMERICAN CHURCHES

AMERICAN CHURCHES

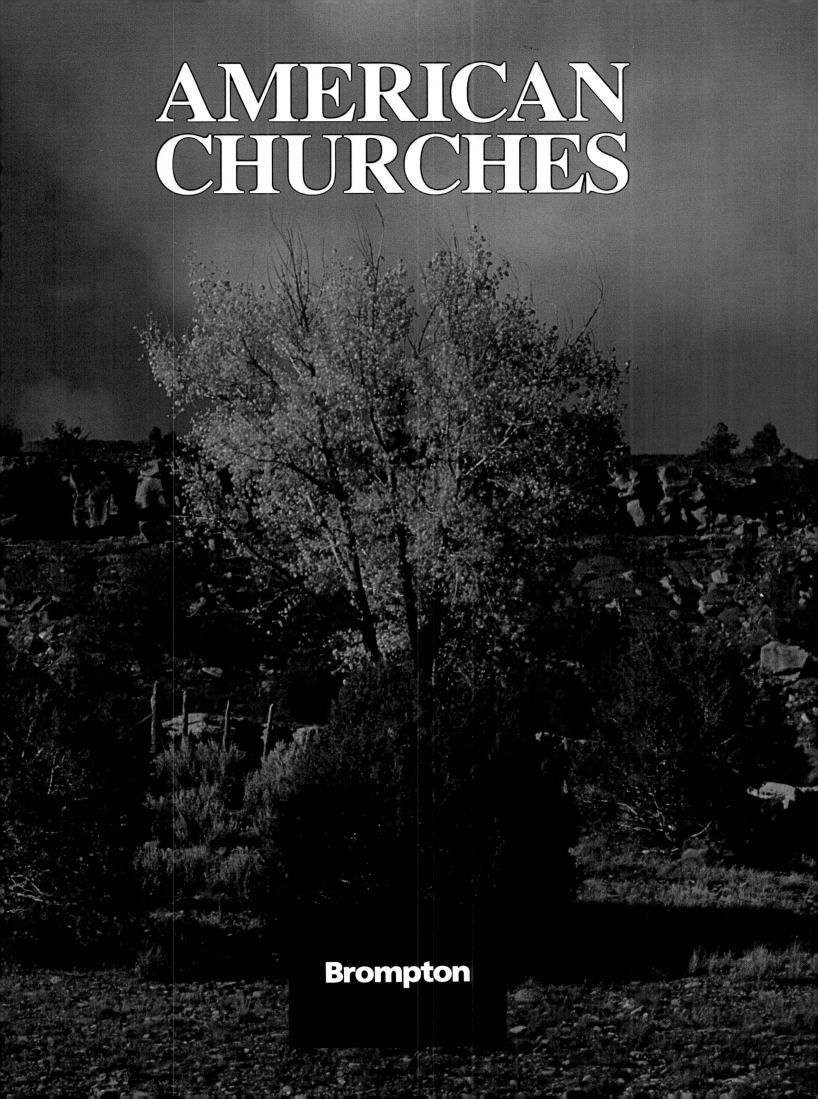

Brompton

First published in 1989 by
Brompton Books Corp
15 Sherwood Place
Greenwich, CT 06830

ISBN 0 86124 543 1

Printed in Hong Kong

Editor's Note

It should be noted that hymns, wherever they appear in this text, have been set as poems, which indeed they are. We find that this treatment emphasizes the meaning of the words, and enhances the reader's appreciation of the various truths expressed.

When it is noted that a text is 'from' a larger, pre-existing text, more often than not we have had to adapt such a text to our special limitations, with the hope — and belief — that those encountering such text will be edified nonetheless.

Designed by Ruth DeJauregui
Edited and Captioned by Timothy Jacobs

Page 1: In South Dakota, a classic aspect of church architecture is seen in this edifice, its tall steeple lifting the symbol of the faith into the sky.

Pages 2–3: The simplicity of this old church in Juanita, Colorado is typical of many places of worship that were built on the American Frontier.

Photo Credits

CONTENTS

INTRODUCTION 6
A Return
by Jacobs Timmons 6

THE NORTHEAST 8
Battle Hymn of the Republic
by Julia Ward Howe 11
Psalm 24 11
Psalm 150 12
Now Doth the Sun Ascend the Sky
Anonymous 15
The Parson's Prayer
by Ralph S Cushman 16
II Corinthians 6:1 – 6,10 21
I Love Thy Kingdom, Lord
by Timothy Dwight 22
Isaiah 55:3, 6 – 7 22
I Heard the Bells
by Henry Wadsworth Longfellow 24
In the House Whose Walls With Life
by Thomas Swenson 27
Falling Leaves
by Benjamin F Brown 29
In Music's Sweetest Strains
Anonymous 33
In the Christian's Home in Glory
by William Hunter 35
In the Bleak Midwinter
by Christina Georgina Rossetti 36
Sun of My Soul
by John Keble 39
John 3:16 – 21 40
Psalm 18:2 – 6 41
Christ is Made the Sure Foundation
trans by Rev JM Neale 43
My Prayer
by Toyohiko Kagawa 44

THE SOUTH 46
The Narrow Path to Home
by Andrew Jacobs 49
Psalm 84 51
If All the Stars
by Andrew Jacobs 51
Till He Come, O Let the Words
by Edward H Bikersteth 53
Ephesians 2:13 – 22 56
Isaiah 40:22, 25 59
Matthew 3:1 – 2, 5 – 6 and
Acts 10:46 – 48 60
The Little Brown Church in the Vale
by William Pitts 63
When I Went Up the Church's Tower
by Oscar Jay Adams 65

Hymn for a Church
by Andrews Norton 66
Psalm 23 70
Joyful, Joyful We Adore Thee
by Henry Van Dyke 72
Deliverance
by Andrew Jacobs 74

THE GREAT LAKES 76
Matthew 7:21 – 29 78
Matthew 7:7 – 20 81
Life, Death and Congregation
by Andrew Jacobs 83
I Would Not Live Always
by William Augustus Muhlenberg 85

THE GREAT PLAINS 86
Hail, Queen of Heaven
by Rev Dr Lingard 88
The Temple of the Prairie
by EM Duffield 91
Restoration of a Church
Anonymous 95
The House is Not for Me
by George MacDonald 96
Matthew 8:8, 19 and 20 97

THE SOUTHWEST 98
O Spirit of the Living God
by Rev W Statham 100
Acts 2:17 – 18, 21, 38 – 42,
46 – 47 103
The Church's One Foundation
by Samuel J Stone 106
The Indian
by MA Vroman 108 – 112

THE MOUNTAIN WEST 114
Amazing Grace
by John Newton 116
Your House
by Andrew Jacobs 118
God's Temples
by Edith D Osborne 121
Psalm 98 122
Waiting for the Coming of
Our Lord Jesus Christ
by Henry Smart 127
John 10:1 – 6 127
Jesus, Where'er Thy People Meet
by William Cowper 128

Appreciation and Criticisms of
the Work of Charles Dickens
by GK Chesterton 130
Remember, Holy Mary
from a Slovak hymnal 130
The Master's Hand
by MA Vroman 135
John 3:31 – 3 6 136
The First Meeting
by George MacDonald 136

THE FAR NORTH 138
Psalm 132:4 – 16 140
Ephesians 5:25 – 33 142
I Timothy 3:14 – 16 145
Haggai 2:3 – 9 146

THE PACIFIC COAST 148
Festival of a Dedication of a Church
trans by Rev JM Neale 151
Revealed to Babes
by George MacDonald 152
The Word, Descending From Above
by Rev E Caswall 155
The Priest of Spring
by GK Chesterton 157
The First and Present Christians
by Andrew Jacobs 158
Psalm 90:1 – 4, 10 and 12 – 17 160
Psalm 27:1 – 6 163
Faith of Our Fathers
by Father Faber 164
Psalm 116 167
As Fades the Glowing Orb of Day
trans by TJ Potter 168
I Kings 6:1 – 7 and John
10:7 – 11, 22 – 23 172
Love Divine
by Rev C Wesley 174
Micah 4:1 – 8 176
The City Upon the Hill
from the Book of Matthew 177
Psalm 136 and Psalm 135:1 – 7,
9 – 14, 19 – 21 179
Pleasant Are Thy Courts
by Rev Francis H Lyte 180
O Gladsome Light
Orthodox hymn 182
Psalm 134 and Luke 1:30 – 35, and
46 – 55 183
Isaiah 56:6 – 8 and
Psalm 51:17 – 18 185
Psalm 91:1 – 9 186
Prayer
by MA Vroman 188 – 190

INTRODUCTION

Who among us is not familiar with the little white church that is set in the middle of town? Or for that matter, who can *ignore* the stately cathedral that occupies its prominent square on the edge of Main Street's business district?

My own fascination with church architecture began when I was a college student, taking a course in — of all things — Byzantine architecture. Soon enough, my attention was also drawn to the pristine, Puritan austerities of the white clapboard Baptist church on the block where I lived.

Consider, for instance, the typical Roman Catholic cathedral, with all its neo-Gothic impressiveness. At the center of this design, the floor plan is a cross — and the clerestory windows insure that 'all the light comes down from above.'

The lines of most Protestant churches represent a stylistic variety that includes the built-in symbology of the above — at one end of the spectrum — to the simple lines and pristine color scheme of that very 'little white church' with which we started this essay.

Add to this the truly astonishing, iconic complexity of many Eastern Orthodox churches — with their onion domes symbolizing candles held up to heaven, a certain number of domes further symbolizing religious themes such as the Holy Trinity, the Twelve Apostles and even the Oneness of the Church — and one finds oneself presented with a multiplicity of architectural graces that are the fruits of a vital tradition.

When I go back to my home town, the road descending the mountainside affords me an excellent panorama that includes three local landmarks — up on the far hill is white-on-white Fairview Baptist Church; at the city line is Trinity Episcopal, with its tall, vented bell tower; and in the center of town, I see the rosette window and twin spires of Saint Joseph's Roman Catholic Church.

Though I've traveled far and wide, these sights rest fondly in my heart. Oh, I'm well acquainted with marvels and wonders — the awesome sense of power conveyed by that masterpiece of cathedrals, Notre Dame in Paris — and I've found my senses reeling in the Byzantine splendor of San Vitale in Ravenna.

But the true test of my appreciation — expertise — is the sense of joy and wonder that is there for me, in the churches I find at home.

— Brian Bevilacqua

A RETURN

In the falling leaves and familiar avenues, I found the tall, white church. Its steeple far above that tolled away the years, stood as I stood: still here, after decades of existence.

Ah, how I love that church, even as I loved it then, when, as a child, I walked the leaf-strewn streets on my way to Bible class. Everything was fresher, more alive, when I walked to Bible class.

And so, I return, and at last I feel my footing — once again — on the church-front stair, as the first notes of the organ pipes play a welcome song.

— Jacob Timmons

Below: Pipe organs such as this, in St George's Church in Halifax, Nova Scotia, have enabled 'man to praise God mightily.' Their music has drawn many of the devout to such as the pristine edifice at *right*, in Massachusetts.

THE NORTHEAST

BATTLE HYMN OF THE REPUBLIC

Mine eyes have seen the glory of the coming of the Lord;
  He is trampling out the vintage
  where the grapes of wrath are stored;
He hath loosed the fateful lightning
  of his terrible swift sword;
  His truth is marching on.

I have seen him in the watchfires
  of a hundred circling camps;
  They have builded him an altar
  in the evening dews and damps;
I can read his righteous sentence
  by the dim and flaring lamps,
  His day is marching on.

He has sounded forth the trumpet that shall never call retreat;
  He is sifting out the hearts of men
  before his judgment seat;
O be swift, my soul, to answer him; be jubilant, my feet!
  Our God is marching on.

In the beauty of the lilies Christ was born across the sea,
  With a glory in his bosom that transfigures you and me;
As he died to make men holy, let us die to make men free!
  While God is marching on.

—Julia Ward Howe

PSALM 24

The earth is the Lord's, and the fullness thereof; the world, and they that dwell therein.

For he hath founded it upon the seas, and established it upon the floods.

Who shall ascend into the hill of the Lord? Or who shall stand in his holy place?

He that hath clean hands, and a pure heart; who hath not lifted up his soul unto vanity, nor sworn deceitfully.

He shall receive the blessing from the Lord, and righteousness from the God of his salvation.

This is the generation of them that seek him, that seek thy face, O Jacob. Selah.

Lift up your heads, O ye gates; and be ye lifted up, ye everlasting doors; and the King of glory shall come in.

Who is the King of glory? The Lord strong and mighty, the Lord mighty in battle.

Lift up your heads, O ye gates; even lift them up, ye everlasting doors; and the King of glory shall come in.

Who is this King of glory? The Lord of hosts, he is the King of glory. Selah.

He hath sounded forth the trumpet . . . and the lights of historic Union Church impart a golden glow to a wintery scene *on the previous pages*. This church was built in 1853, and is a classic example of simple, rectangular 'New England meeting house' architecture. *At left*, in the midst of earth's fullness, is this historic place of worship in Vermont. Note the pillared portico of this Greek Revival church, emphatically a 'temple' of worship.

PSALM 150

Praise ye the Lord. Praise God in his sanctuary: praise him in the firmament of his power.

Praise him for his mighty acts: praise him according to his excellent greatness.

Praise him with the sound of the trumpet: praise him with the psaltery and harp.

Praise him with the timbrel and dance: praise him with stringed instruments and organs.

Praise him upon the loud cymbals: praise him upon the high sounding cymbals.

Let every thing that hath breath praise the Lord. Praise ye the Lord.

Above: Gladness and thanksgiving at a church fair in Newbury, Vermont. The church is built in the capacious 'meeting house' style that facilitates its intended role as center of community activity. *At right:* This stately and well-preserved brick church awaits its congregation. The two-tiered steeple once held bells; chimes are now the fashion. The glass upper steeple, or 'lantern,' contains a light, to 'light the way' for the faithful at night.

NOW DOTH THE SUN
ASCEND THE SKY

Now doth the sun ascend the sky,
    And wake creation with its ray;
Be present with us, Lord most high;
    Through all the actions of the day.
Keep us eternal, Lord, this day,
    From every sinful passion free;
Grant us in all we do or say,
    In all our thoughts to honor Thee,
Grant us in all we do or say,
    In all our thoughts to honor Thee.

Upon our fainting soul distill,
    The grace of Thy celestial dew;
Let no fresh snare to sin beguile,
    No former sin revive anew.
Teach us to knock at heaven's high door,
    Teach us the prize of life to win;
Teach us all evil to abhor,
    And purify ourselves within,
Teach us all evil to abhor,
    And purify ourselves within.

— *Anonymous*

Cathedrals emulate the heavenly hierarchy. Twin spires represent Sts Peter and Paul.
At left is St Patrick's in New York City — opened in 1877 and dedicated in 1879.
At right and *above* are views of Notre Dame in Montreal.

THE PARSON'S PRAYER

I do not ask
That crowds may throng the temple,
   That standing room be priced:
I only ask that as I voice the message
   They may see Christ!

I do not ask
For churchly pomp or pageant
   Or music such as wealth alone can buy:
I only ask that as I voice the message
   He may be nigh!

I do not ask
That men may sound my praises;
   Or headlines spread my name abroad:
I only pray that as I voice the message
   Hearts may find God!

I do not ask
For earthly place or laurel,
   Or of this world's distinctions any part:
I only ask when I have voiced the message
   My Savior's heart!

—Ralph S Cushman

These pages: St George's church in Halifax, Nova Scotia. Its round nave echoes the early 'Christianizing' of Greek temples, and symbolizes the oneness of the Church. *Overleaf:* Old First Church in Bennington, Vermont — it has a pronounced Protestant spareness for a church of its considerable size.

II CORINTHIANS 6:1 – 6, 10

We then as workers together with him, beseech you also that ye receive not the grace of God in vain.

(For he saith, I have heard thee in a time accepted, and in the day of salvation have I succored thee; behold, now is the accepted time; behold, now is the day of salvation.)

Giving no offense in any thing, that the ministry be not blamed:

But in all things proving ourselves as the ministers of God, in much patience, in afflictions, in necessities, in distresses,

In stripes, in imprisonments, in tumults, in labors, in watchings, in fastings;

By pureness, by knowledge, by long suffering, by kindness, by the Holy Ghost, by love unfeigned,

As sorrowful, yet always rejoicing; as poor, yet making many rich; as having nothing, and yet possessing all things.

At left is the Orthodox church at Holy Trinity Monastery in New York. *Above* is the chapel of a 'skete,' or small monastic community affiliated with the larger monastery. Onion domes are 'candles lit to heaven'—one stands for Christ, the head of the church; three, the Holy Trinity; five, Christ and the four Evangelists; seven, the sacraments; nine, the orders of angels; and 13, Christ and His apostles. Monks live to maintain a pure, full, Christianity.

I LOVE THY KINGDOM, LORD

I love thy kingdom, Lord,
  The house of thine abode,
The church our blest Redeemer saved
  With his own precious blood.

For her my tears shall fall;
  For her my prayers ascend;
To her my cares and toils be given,
  Till toils and cares shall end.

Beyond my highest joy
  I prize her heavenly ways,
Her sweet communion, solemn vows,
  Her hymns of love and praise.

Sure as the truth shall last,
  To Zion shall be given
The brightest glories earth can yield,
  And brighter bliss of heaven.

— Timothy Dwight

ISAIAH 55:3, 6 – 7

Incline your ear, and come unto me; hear, and your soul shall live; and I will make an everlasting covenant with you . . .

Seek ye the Lord while he may be found, call ye upon him while he is near:

Let the wicked forsake his way, and the unrighteous man his thought: and let him return unto the Lord, and he will have mercy upon him; and to our God, for he will abundantly pardon.

For my thoughts are not your thoughts, neither are your ways my ways, saith the Lord.

For as the heavens are higher than the earth, so are my ways higher than your ways, and my thoughts than your thoughts.

For as the rain cometh down, and the snow from heaven, and returneth not thither, but watereth the earth, and maketh it bring forth and bud, that it may give seed to the sower, and bread to the eater:

So shall my word be that goeth forth out of my mouth: it shall not return unto me void, but it shall accomplish that which I please, and it shall prosper in the thing whereto I sent it.

At right: The purity of a winter landscape echoes the purity of faith. This small New England church bears a steeple of the 'watch tower' type, symbolic of the Christian admonition to await the coming of the Lord, and to maintain vigilance in this life. The clapboard sides of this edifice, brilliantly reflecting light, proclaim as loudly as its bell (now removed) once did.

I HEARD THE BELLS

I heard the bells on Christmas day
Their old familiar carols play,
And wild and sweet the words repeat
Of peace on earth, good will to men.

And thought how, as the day had come,
The belfries of all Christendom
Had rolled along the unbroken song
Of peace on earth, good will to men.

And in despair I bowed my head:
'There is no peace on earth,' I said:
'For hate is strong, and mocks the song
Of peace on earth, good will to men.'

Then pealed the bells more loud and deep
'God is not dead, nor doth he sleep;
The wrong shall fail, the right prevail,
With peace on earth, good will to men.'

Till, ringing, singing on its way,
The world revolved from night to day,
A voice, a chime, a chant sublime,
Of peace on earth, good will to men.

—Henry Wadsworth Longfellow

Above: The steep-sloped roof of St George's Episcopal Church in Scenectady, Delaware, hearkens to another era, as does its large bell tower (which long ago would have stood detached), the pealing of whose bells would recall an age before the advent of 'chimes.' The pure resonance of bellringing is said to 'cleanse the air,' and echoes a sense of the otherworldly, just as the steeple *at right,* lifting its cross on high, proclaims the truth of Christ.

IN THE HOUSE WHOSE
WALLS WITH LIFE

No more the sea's exulting roar
  Could echo in my ears
And Swedish woodland thickets
  were hid, far gone in years—
My life's sad state had carried me
  beyond my childhood fears:
It left me cold, with empty heart
  in ruin, and pain, and tears.

But then before the clear blue sky
  could swallow my last breath,
A kindly word from Uncle Lars
  rescued me from death.
'Tom,' he said, 'There is a place
  where you can find you rest.
The House of the Almighty Lord—
  lay your head upon His breast.'

And so I did, and to this day
  his aged smile comes to mind,
When lifting up my voice in prayer
  seeing clearly—who am so often blind—
Oh, it's no end of troubles
  but it does make one more kind:
It's the true testing of manhood
  in the house whose walls with life are lined.

— Thomas Swenson

At left: Trinity Old Swedes Church in Wilmington, Delaware evidences a spare and simple design, with a bell tower that was, apparently, a later addition. The custom of burying the dead near the church has to do with the notion of 'hallowed ground.'

Above is the interior of Gloucester, New Jersey's King of Sweden Church, whose barrel-vault ceiling and plain lines resemble those of an ancient Swedish 'great hall,' where the chieftain held his court.

FALLING LEAVES

Falling leaves, falling leaves,
    Back to earth,
Back to the source that gave them birth.
So do we, life's voyage past,
Take down the sails, release the mast,
And willing, cross the storm-lashed beach
Our Father's welcome home to reach.

— *Benjamin F Brown*

At left, amidst a falling-leaf display of the impermanence of earthly life, the steep gables of this church point upward to the hope that those who have gone on — as *at right* — have found heaven. *Above:* The old Sudbury Meeting House church, in Vermont. *Overleaf:* Christ Church, in New Brunswick.

IN MUSIC'S SWEETEST STRAINS

In music's sweetest strains we'll sing;
  Our notes to God we'll raise;
And make His sacred temple ring,
  With hymns of love and praise;
And make His sacred temple ring,
  With hymns of love and praise.

Our tongues hosannas shall proclaim;
  Our hearts devoutly pray;
Each morning and each evening theme,
  Shall echo through the day;
Each morning and each evening theme,
  Shall echo through the day.

In God's own house we'll sing His praise,
  For there His glory dwells;
To Heav'n our hearts and songs we'll raise,
  In sweetest canticles,
To Heav'n our heart and songs we'll raise,
  In sweetest canticles.

As long as we have life and breath,
  Our Maker we will praise;
And when our voice expires in death,
  Death will perfect our lays;
And when our voice expires in death,
  Death will perfect our lays.

— Anonymous

At left: The bells of Eglise St Gregoire (Church of St Gregory) refresh the parishioners of Nicolet, Quebec with holy themes. Note the symbology of triple entrance doors; an extended, tripart facade that underlies the classical entablature; and the three crosses (with a fourth inconspicuous at the rear). *Above, both:* A stained glass window and a votive lamp contribute to the light inside Eglise de la Purification in Repentigny, Quebec.

IN THE CHRISTIAN'S HOME
IN GLORY

In the Christian's home in glory,
    There remains a land of rest;
There my Savior's gone before me,
    To fulfill my soul's request.

He is fitting up my mansion,
    Which eternally shall stand,
For my stay shall not be transient,
    In that holy, happy land.

Pain and sickness ne'er shall enter,
    Grief nor woe my lot shall share;
But, in that celestial center,
    I a crown of life shall wear.

Death itself shall then be vanquished,
    And his sting shall be withdrawn;
Shout for gladness, oh, ye ransomed!
    Hail with joy the rising morn.

— *William Hunter*

At left, we see an example of modified 'meeting house' church architecture, with the clock on the bell tower serving to mark time both to inform, and to symbolically *remind,* the congregation. The church *above,* in Stock Cove, Newfoundland, departs from the linear norm, with its side-mounted narthex and bell tower, and is also quite distinctive with its bold trimwork and double lancet windows, which reveal ancient — as well as rustic — influences.

IN THE BLEAK MIDWINTER

In the bleak midwinter
  Frosty wind made moan,
Earth stood hard as iron,
  Water like a stone;
Snow had fallen, snow on snow.
  Snow on snow,
In the bleak midwinter
  Long ago.

Our God, Heaven cannot hold Him,
  Nor earth sustain;
Heaven and earth shall flee away
  When He comes to reign:
In the bleak midwinter
  A stable stall sufficed
The Lord God Almighty
  Jesus Christ.

Enough for Him, whom cherubim
  Worship night and day,
A breastful of milk
  And a mangerful of hay;
Enough for Him, whom angels
  Fall down before,
The ox and ass and camel
  Which adore.

Angels and archangels
  May have gathered there,
Cherubim and seraphim
  Thronged the air;
But only His mother
  In her maiden bliss
Worshipped the Beloved
  With a kiss.

What can I give Him,
  Poor as I am?
If I were a shepherd
  I would bring a lamb,
If I were a Wise Man
  I would do my part,
Yet what I can I give Him,
  Give my heart.

—*Christina Georgina Rossetti*

At right: The mellow sunlight brings warmth to the walls of this New England church. Built in the two-story 'meeting house' style, it is a structure built to be heart of activity for a devout and thriving community. Although indigenous to New England, this type of construction can be found in all areas of North America. The concept of making the church the center of community activity goes all the way back to the writings of Paul, who exhorted Christians to live in community with one another, and has traditionally been—until very recently—the basis for civic planning. It survives in its purest form in monastic communities, where the teachings of Christ define the parameters of life. The present form of meeting hall church arose out of the reformative-minded Protestant settlements in colonial North America. Feeling that the established churches had gone too far in the way of adornment, these early immigrants sought to propound the maximum of plainness and rationalist utility, even in their places of worship.

SUN OF MY SOUL

When the soft dews of kindly sleep
My wearied eyelids gently steep,
Be my last thought how sweet to rest
Forever on my Savior's breast,

Abide with me from morn till eve,
For without Thee I cannot live;
Abide with me when night is nigh,
For without Thee I dare not die.

If some poor wandering child of Thine
Has spurned today the Voice Divine,
Now, Lord, the gracious work begin,
Let him no more lie down in sin.

Come near and bless us when we wake,
Ere through the world our way we take,
Till in the ocean of Thy love,
We lose ourselves in heaven above.

— *John Keble*

Tradition dictates that the church entrance should open to the west, with the altar to the east, so that congregations face the waxing, not the waning, light. St Paul's Church, *above*, with its clapboard siding and classical entablature, makes an interesting contrast to the ruggedly elegant natural stone construction of the Church of the Messiah, *at left*. The former is in Halifax, Nova Scotia, and the latter is in Sabrevois, Quebec.

JOHN 3:16 – 21

For God so loved the world, that he gave his only begotten Son, that whosoever believeth in him should not perish, but have everlasting life.

For God sent not his Son into the world to condemn the world; but that the world through him might be saved.

He that believeth on him is not condemned; but he that believeth not is condemned already; because he hath not believed in the name of the only begotten Son of God.

And this is the condemnation, that light is come into the world, and men loved darkness rather than light, because their deeds were evil.

For every one that doeth evil hateth the light, neither cometh to the light, lest his deeds should be reproved.

But he that doeth truth cometh to the light, that his deeds may be made manifest, that they are wrought in God.

PSALM 18:2–6

. . . The Lord is my rock, and my fortress, and my deliverer; my God, my strength, in whom I will trust; my buckler, and the horn of my salvation, and my high tower.

I will call upon the Lord, who is worthy to be praised: so shall I be saved from mine enemies.

The sorrows of death compassed me, and the floods of ungodly men made me afraid.

The sorrows of hell compassed me about: the snares of death prevented me.

In my distress I called upon the Lord, and cried unto my God: he heard my voice out of his temple, and my cry came before him . . . .

Churches and cemeteries go together as does the Christian faith and the afterlife. Christian architecture depicts not only earthly transience and humility, but also the eternal glory of God—which begets simplicity in some cases, and complexity in others. *Above left:* A very simple Welsh tract church in Delaware. *Above:* The more complex Old Covenanter's Church in Grand Pre, Nova Scotia. See also pages 14–15, 20–25 and 28–29 for more examples.

CHRIST IS MADE THE SURE FOUNDATION

Christ is made the sure foundation,
   Christ the head and cornerstone,
Chosen of the Lord, and precious,
   Binding all the church in one.

To this temple, where we call thee,
   Come, O Lord of hosts, today:
With thy wonted loving kindness
   Hear thy people as they pray.

Here vouchsafe to all thy servants
   What they ask of thee to gain,
What they gain from thee forever
   With the blessed to retain.

Laud and honor to the Father,
   Laud and honor to the Son,
Laud and honor to the Spirit,
   Ever Three and ever One.

— *Rev JM Neale, translator*

At left: United Church, in Jordan Falls, Nova Scotia. Note the small flower windows on the bell tower, and their unusual counterparts at the base of the steeple. On both this and Minudie United Church *(above)*, located in the same province, the windows have the pointed tips common to Gothic church windows. Note the differences in treatment of the two clapboard-sided buildings, which are of similar configuration and have like denominational foundation.

MY PRAYER

In the clear morning
I have climbed the hill.

Smoke from the factories
Rolls west to east
Across the huge red sun.

A train puffs past
Through tiny, far-off fields.
Bright buds are everywhere.

  God of the hills,
  The smoke,
  The sun,
The growing grain,
I cannot word my prayer.

God . . . green things . . .
Green things . . . God . . .
Lord of each little leaf
  On every tree
Lord of the clouds that drift
  Far out to sea,
  I thank Thee
That Thou has shown
  Jesus
  To me.

God,
I pray
That Thou wilt take
Evil away. Amen.

— *Toyohiko Kagawa*

At left: Derived from a deep folk tradition, ornately carved trimwork adorns a beautiful shuttered church in Sterling, Massachusetts. *Above:* Note the mullioned window and auxiliary chapels of this Round Lake, New York, church. *At right:* The neo-Gothic spires of St Patrick's make a strong contrast against the secular glare of contemporary New York City.

THE NARROW PATH TO HOME

It's the narrow path to home
and I walk it when I roam
alone with God, whose edicts I descry
in the heart and voice and eye
of the many friends I meet
in fellowship so sweet

When all are gathered
  in our one true home
Beneath a warm and cloudless sky.

It's the narrow path to home
and I walk it as I roam
alone with God, who teaches me
the truth, and then from falsehood how to see

The thorny way of life
in peace, resolving strife

Wherever we are gathered
  under roof or bright blue sky —
His spirit shows us how to be.

— *Andrew Jacobs*

Previous pages: First Baptist Church in Welaka, Florida, has a tin roof against the elements, an elegant porch, and a flowering field to line the congregation's way as they walk to church. *At left:* A historic church in Richmond, Virginia, with a compound steeple, eight-pane windows and a brick walkway. *Above left:* Alpha and omega in stained glass; and *above right*, an interior view of pews and glasswork — from St John's Church, also in Richmond.

PSALM 84

How amiable are thy tabernacles, O Lord of hosts!

My soul longeth, yea, even fainteth for the courts of the Lord; my heart and my flesh crieth out for the living God.

Yea, the sparrow hath found a house, and the swallow a nest for herself, where she may lay her young, even thine altars, O Lord of hosts, my King, and my God.

Blessed are they that dwell in thy house: they will be still praising thee. Selah.

Blessed the man whose strength is in thee; in whose heart are the ways of them,

Who passing through the valley of Baca make it a well; the rain also filleth the pools.

They go from strength to strength, every one of them in Zion appeareth before God.

O Lord God of hosts, hear my prayer: give ear, O God of Jacob. Selah.

Behold, O God our shield, and look upon the face of thine anointed.

For a day in thy courts is better than a thousand. I had rather be a doorkeeper in the house of my God, than to dwell in the tents of wickedness.

For the Lord God a sun and shield: the Lord will give grace and glory: no good will he withhold from them that walk uprightly.

O Lord of hosts, blessed the man that trusteth in thee.

IF ALL THE STARS

If all the stars fell from heaven,
  and the hands of every saint —
  beset by friend and foe
  for the sake of immortal God —
sent up praises to the Highest,

Even then, would be excuses
  that humility is hard, and
  lowliness not easy,
  though it require you refrain
    against your many passions.

The roofs and spires of God's houses
  rise to tell us of this mystery,
  and so, we too, within ourselves,
  by calming down, by staying still
rise up from our foundations to the sky,

And reaching higher still,
  with hands of prayer
Gain what strength we need
  with hands of prayer.

Andrew Jacobs

At left: Flagler Presbyterian, in Florida. Domes date back to ancient times, when they were made of pottery 'honeycomb,' for lightweight strength. They provide a certain mystic sense of interior elevation and lighting, and symbolize the heavenly realm. Note the porticoed windows under the central dome.

TILL HE COME, O LET THE WORDS

'Till he come,' O let the words
  Linger on the trembling chords;
Let the little while between
  In their golden light be seen;
Let us think how heav'n and home
  Lie beyond that 'Till he come.'

Clouds and conflicts round us press;
  Would we have one sorrow less?
All the sharpness of the cross,
  All that tells the world is loss;
Death and darkness and the tomb,
  Only whisper, 'Till he come.'

See, the feast of love is spread:
  Drink the wine, and break the bread;
Sweet memorials — till the Lord
  Call us round his heav'nly board;
Some from earth, from glory some:
  Severed only 'Till he come.'

— Edward H Bikersteth

At left: Wheel-flowers (symbolizing the oneness of the fruits of Christ) and cruciform stars (symbolizing heaven and earth come together in Christ) adorn the glasswork behind the communion altar of a church in Georgia. *Above:* An array of stained glass windows gather the golden sunlight into this Methodist Church. *Overleaf:* A modern rural chapel, with gothic arches and impressionistic stained glass. Sweeping rooflines mimic the flight of the soul.

EPHESIANS 2:13–22

But now in Christ Jesus ye who sometimes were far off are made nigh by the blood of Christ.

For he is our peace, who hath made both one, and hath broken down the middle wall of partition between us;

Having abolished in his flesh the enmity, even the law of commandments contained in ordinances; for to make in himself of twain one new man, so making peace:

And that he might reconcile both unto God in one body by the cross, having slain the enmity thereby;

And came and preached peace to you which were afar off, and to them that were nigh.

For through him we both have access by one Spirit unto the Father.

Now therefore ye are no more strangers and foreigners, but fellow citizens with the saints, and of the household of God;

And are built up on the foundation of the apostles and prophets, Jesus Christ himself being the chief cornerstone.

In whom all the building fitly framed together groweth unto a holy temple in the Lord:

In whom ye also are builded together for a habitation of God through the Spirit.

At right: The Cathedral of St Augustine, in St Augustine, Florida. Note the pottery-tile roof, and the cruciform sidewalk that leads to the figure of Father Camps *(above)*, who is depicted aiding Minorcan immigrants who were, in the days of the early settling of the area, tricked into working under virtual slavery. Father Camps brought spiritual strength to them in their distress.

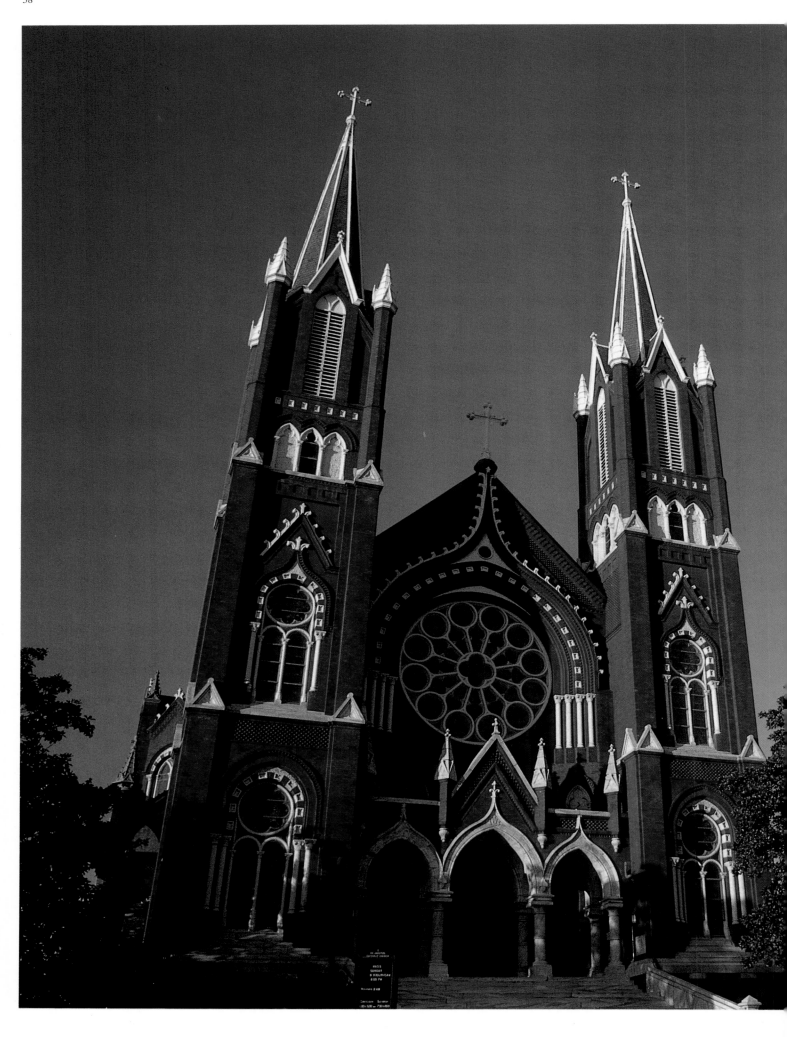

ISAIAH 40:22, 25

It is he that sitteth upon the circle of the earth . . . that stretcheth out the heavens as a curtain, and spreadeth them out as a tent to dwell in . . .

To whom then shall ye liken me, or shall I be equal? Saith the Holy One.

Religious architecture abounds with parallels and harmonies of motifs in its appointed task to create structures which reflect, intimate and bear fruit of the glory of God. *At left:* St Joseph's Catholic Church, in Macon, Georgia has classic Gothic verticality, and its rose window, symbolizing abundant wholeness, is echoed on either side by smaller portals. Portico windows high on either belltower lead one to look higher, to the louvered steeple, where the sound of bells peal forth the hours, calling the people to prayer. *Above:* False buttresses, a tripart mullioned window and the Star of Bethlehem adorn the facade of this Baptist church in Mississippi.

MATTHEW 3:1 – 2, 5 – 6,
and ACTS 10:46 – 48

. . . In those days came John the Baptist, preaching in the wilderness of Judea,

And saying Repent ye, for the Kingdom of Heaven is at hand. . . . Then went out to him Jerusalem, and all Judea, and all the region about Jordan,

And were baptized of him in Jordan, confessing their sins.

. . . Then answered Peter, Can any man forbid water, that these should not be baptized, which have received the Holy Ghost as well as we?

And he commanded them to be baptized in the name of the Lord . . .

Above: This old, wilderness Catholic church, with its three windows and single entrance, does much symbolically with a very simple architecture. It's located in Jefferson County, Mississippi. Stained glass work, such as that shown *at right* (see also page 41), often depicts pious themes from the past. Here, we see the fruit of missionary endeavor in the baptism of the Indian maiden, Pocahontas. This window is at St John's Church in Richmond, Virginia.

THE LITTLE BROWN
CHURCH IN THE VALE

Oh come to the church
   in the wild wood,
come to the church
   in the vale.
For no place is so dear
   to my childhood
as the little brown church
   in the vale.

— William Pitts

On these pages: Exterior and interior views of Moss Hill Church, in De Funiak Springs, Florida—the oldest Methodist church in the United States. Set on brick pylons for protection from flooding, it has stood the test of Florida's elements over the years. Note the two front doors, typical in early American churches. Its plank interior, including an extremely straightforward pulpit, has been well preserved. While the original 'Little Brown Church in the Vale' is on page 94, the church on these pages has been that very item for *its* congregations, over many years of service.

65

from
WHEN I WENT UP
THE CHURCH'S TOWER

When I went up the church's tower,
The church clock rang out the hour;
The restless organ far below
Sent tides of music to and fro,
That rolled through nave and angel choir,
Whose builder knew what lines inspire,
And filled the chamber's space profound
With climbing waves of glorious sound,
As I went up the church's tower
That time the chimes gave forth the hour.

— *Oscar Jay Adams*

At left: A church lamp hangs like a pendulum anchored in a Maltese cross of braces.
Above: An impressively monumental Victorian-era church in Mississippi. *At right:*
A sign proclaiming the mystical foundation of a church.

HYMN FOR A CHURCH

Where ancient forests round us spread,
　Where bends the cataract's ocean-fall,
On the lone mountain's silent head,
　There are thy temples, God of all!

Beneath the dark-blue, midnight arch,
　Whence myriad suns pour down their rays,
Where planets trace their ceaseless march,
　Father! we worship as we gaze.

The tombs thine altars are; for there,
　When earthly loves and hopes have fled,
To thee ascends the spirit's prayer,
　Thou God of the immortal dead.

All space is holy; for all space
　Is filled by thee; but human thought
Burns clearer in some chosen place,
　Where thy own words of love are taught.

Here be they taught; and may we know
　That faith thy servants knew of old;
Which onward bears through weal and woe,
　Till Death the gates of heaven unfold!

Nor we alone; may those whose brow
　Shows yet no trace of human cares,
Hereafter stand where we do now,
　And raise to thee still holier prayers!

— *Andrews Norton*

Above: We look through the blossoms toward Christ Church in Alexandria, Virginia. It's an outstanding example of early American church architecture, with its basic box frame structure housing a wealth of ecclesiastical detail, as can be seen from the interior *at right.* Note the small-paned window, the silver candelabra, and the Nicene Creed. *Overleaf:* A beautiful little brick church, and its brick-walled churchyard, in Petersburg, Virginia.

PSALM 23

The Lord is my shepherd: I shall not want.

He maketh me to lie down in green pastures: he leadeth me beside the still waters.

He restoreth my soul: he leadeth me in the paths of righteousness for his name's sake.

Yea, though I walk through the valley of the shadow of death, I will fear no evil: for thou art with me; thy rod and thy staff, they comfort me.

Thou preparest a table before me in the presence of mine enemies: thou anointest my head with oil; my cup runneth over.

Surely goodness and mercy shall follow me all the days of my life; and I will dwell in the house of the Lord forever.

The verdant, agrarian South is one of the best places to find small country churches. *Above* is a country church near Jackson, Mississippi. Note that a wheelchair access has been added to this small structure. Note also that the church, like many in the wetlands, is set on piers for protection against moisture and flooding. *At right* is Bruton Parish Church, one of the oldest Episcopal churches in the US, in continuous service to 'God and man' since 1715.

BRUTON PARISH CHURCH
Services on Sundays & Special Days

One of the oldest Episcopal Churches
in America, this historic building
has been in service to God and Man
continuously since 1715.

OPEN TO VISITORS EVERY DAY

JOYFUL, JOYFUL, WE
ADORE THEE

Joyful, joyful, we adore thee,
  God of glory, Lord of love;
Hearts unfold like flow'rs before thee,
  Hail thee as the sun above.
Melt the clouds of sin and sadness;
  Drive the dark of doubt away;
Giver of immortal gladness,
  Fill us with the light of day!

All thy works with joy surround thee,
  Earth and heav'n reflect thy rays,
Stars and angels sing around thee,
  Center of unbroken praise.
Field and forest, vale and mountain,
  Bloss'ming meadow, flashing sea,
Chanting bird and flowing fountain,
  Call us to rejoice in thee.

Thou art giving and forgiving,
  Ever blessing, ever blest,
Wellspring of the joy of living,
  Ocean depth of happy rest!
Thou the Father, Christ our Brother—
  All who live in love are thine;
Teach us how to love each other,
  Lift us to the Joy Divine.

Mortals join the mighty chorus,
  Which the morning stars began;
Father love is reigning o'er us,
  Brother love binds man to man.
Ever singing march we onward,
  Victors in the midst of strife;
Joyful music lifts us sunward
  In the triumph song of life.

—Henry Van Dyke

Circular windows such as this, *at right*, have not quite the structural strength of the more massive and more complex rose windows that adorn many cathedrals. Note the cross-bracing that supports the delicate bulk of this particular window. Depicted here is Christ ascended in glory, and his adoring apostles on earth. Note that there are 11 apostles present—minus Judas Iscariot. As shown here, John the Divine, 'the beloved Apostle,' wears robes like those worn by the Savior. This connotes two things—one, that in parallel with the passing of the robe from Elijah to Elishah—and hence the bestowal of a blessed and powerful grace from one to the other—Christ had opened the way for the grace of the Holy Spirit for his disciples; and two, the robe is symbolic of the emulation of Christ that was the essence of the Apostolic life, and remains the desire of every sincere Christian. This circular window is part of St Andrew's Cathedral in Jackson, Mississippi.

DELIVERANCE

This story occurred to me by way of an old man whose great-grandfather had been a missionary guide back in the days when Florida and much of the deep South was still pretty definitely 'missionary territory.'

His great-grandfather was a serious but gentle man whose affability belied the very great inner strength the old man had. The story he passed on to his son, who passed it on to his grandson, goes something like this:

He was traveling with clergy when they were set upon by Indians. The Indians didn't seem to know what to do with the white men once they had them, and the atmosphere had great potential for becoming tense.

A middle-aged minister made it known to his captors that they could keep him if they would let his friends go. To test his mettle, one of the Indians indicated that they sought to make him die slowly and painfully. When the cleric calmly reiterated his offer to be the scapegoat, the Indians smiled, shook hands and patted backs all around, and let everybody go.

When later congratulated on his courage, the 'scapegoat' said that all he'd been doing was praying with all his heart and all his soul that his friends be delivered, and that the Indians would be, too.

— *Andrew Jacobs*

Above left: The oldest church building on its original site in Florida—Old Christ Church, patterned in 1832 on an Anglican design by Sir Christopher Wren. *Above right:* The very old mission chapel of El Nombre de Dios (The Name of God), in St Augustine, Florida, displays typically simple, sturdy missionary construction. Through the door can be seen the Madonna and Child. *At right:* A wilderness monument in Tennessee that needs no explanation.

LAKES

MATTHEW 7:21 – 29

Not every one that saith unto me, Lord, Lord, shall enter into the kingdom of heaven; but he that doeth the will of my Father which is in heaven.

Many will say to me in that day, Lord, Lord, have we not prophesied in thy name? and in thy name have cast out devils? and in thy name done many wonderful works?

And then will I profess unto them, I never knew you: depart from me, ye that work iniquity.

Therefore whosoever heareth these sayings of mine, and doeth them, I will liken him unto a wise man, which built his house upon a rock:

And the rain descended, and the floods came, and the winds blew, and beat upon that house; and it fell not: for it was founded upon a rock.

And every one that heareth these sayings of mine, and doeth them not, shall be likened unto a foolish man, which built his house upon the sand:

And the rain descended, and the floods came, and the winds blew, and beat upon that house; and it fell: and great was the fall of it.

And it came to pass, when Jesus had ended these sayings, the people were astonished at his doctrine:

For he taught them as one having authority, and not as the scribes.

Previous page: St Mark's Anglican Church in Ontario, begun in 1804 and completed in 1810. The nave was rebuilt, after a fire, in 1822. In 1843, the transepts, a chancel and two Gothic Revival pulpits were added. *At right:* Frank Lloyd Wright placed great emphasis on melding architecture into the natural environment—hence, this First Unitarian Church in Madison, Wisconsin; it seems to grow directly out of the hillside. *Above:* On the other hand, some of the Amish prefer to have their worship at the hearth. Therefore, this Illinois Amish school only resembles a church, which points to the interpenetrating influences both of and on ecclesiastical architecture.

1876   1981
Wellington Street United
Church
105th Anniversary

MATTHEW 7:7 – 20

Ask, and it shall be given you; seek, and ye shall find; knock, and it shall be opened unto you:

For every one that asketh receiveth; and he that seeketh findeth; and to him that knocketh it shall be opened.

Or what man is there of you, whom if his son ask bread, will he give him a stone?

Or if he ask a fish, will he give him a serpent?

If ye then, being evil, know how to give good gifts unto your children, how much more shall your Father which is in heaven give good things to them that ask him?

Therefore all things whatsoever ye would that men should do to you, do ye even so to them: for this is the law and the prophets.

Enter ye in at the strait gate: for wide is the gate, and broad is the way, that leadeth to destruction, and many there be which go in thereat:

Because strait is the gate, and narrow is the way, which leadeth unto life, and few there be that find it.

Beware of false prophets, which come to you in sheep's clothing, but inwardly they are ravening wolves.

Ye shall know them by their fruits. Do men gather grapes of thorns, or figs of thistles?

Even so every good tree bringeth forth good fruit; but a corrupt tree bringeth forth evil fruit.

A good tree cannot bring forth evil fruit, neither can a corrupt tree bring forth good fruit.

Every tree that bringeth not forth good fruit is hewn down, and cast into the fire.

Wherefore by their fruits ye shall know them.

At left: The entrance to the ornate, neo-Gothic Wellington Street United Church in London, Ontario, during its 105th Anniversary in 1981. *Above:* A church in Coon Valley, Wisconsin. *At right:* A cross on Bald Nob, in Illinois.

LIFE, DEATH AND CONGREGATION

In the community of the 'called out,' birth, death and worship are all part of the societal 'glue.' Christians view these as integral to a life process that begins in the womb and goes through a profound transition at death, but continues infinitely afterward, provided that one has chosen the 'path of life' and not that of 'death.' Christianity views these concepts as not easily understood to the mortal mind, which thinks entirely 'bodily,' responds to the 'delusions of the body,' and finds its death with that of the body. Christians feel that one should honor one's body as the Temple of the Holy Spirit, but that you shouldn't let it run your life for you. Proper Christian focus is on Christ and His teachings, for only by these can one escape the snare of self-delusion.

Christ, as Son of God, is believed to be the One who defeated death decisively by dying and then resurrecting by the grace of the Holy Spirit, which He had abundantly, as the Son — as in Father, Son and Holy Spirit. While some Christian ascetics practice severe bodily trials, and while fasting is an integral part of many Christian creeds, Christianity is unique in that its primary ingredient is faith in the Trinity, which is not so easy as it sounds. This faith is made 'living' by the active exercise, in one's life, of the commandments of Christ, as given on the Mount of Olives. The two greatest of these commandments were encapsulated by the Master Himself as 'Love God with all thy heart and all thy mind,' and 'Love thy neighbor as thyself.'

Forgiveness and repentance are key ingredients as well, for we are told that 'as thou forgivest, so shalt thou be forgiven,' yet we are admonished not to let others 'tread us underfoot.'

If it sounds difficult, it has been historically shown as both so and not so. Prayer in the name of Jesus Christ is given as the chief enabler for Christians to do 'all things.' Therefore, Christianity would seem to be a mystery easily as ponderable as that of life itself.

The basis for Christian congregation is found in the following, one of Jesus Christ's most well-known (and often misunderstood) statements:

'Where two or more are gathered in My Name, there shall I be.'

— *Andrew Jacobs*

Above: Old Colony Church, in Bishop Hill, Illinois, was built for the needs of a large congregation. *At left:* This pristine, clapboard-sided frame church in Marxville, Wisconsin, stands like a guardian over those 'fallen asleep.'

I WOULD NOT LIVE ALWAYS

I would not live always — live always below!
Oh no, I'll not linger when bidden to go:
The days of our pilgrimage granted us here
Are enough for life's woes, full enough for its cheer:
Would I shrink from the path which the prophets of God,
Apostles, and martyrs, so joyfully trod?
Like a spirit unblest, o'er the earth would I roam,
While brethren and friends are all hastening home?

I would not live always: I ask not to stay
Where storm after storm rises dark o'er the way;
Where seeking for rest we but hover around,
Like the patriarch's bird, and no resting is found;
Where Hope, when she paints her gay bow in the air,
Leaves its brilliance to fade in the night of despair,
And joy's fleeting angel ne'er sheds a glad ray,
Save the gleam of the plumage that bears him away.

I would not live always — thus fettered by sin,
Temptation without and corruption within;
In a moment of strength if I sever the chain,
Scarce the victory's mine, ere I'm captive again;
E'en the rapture of pardon is mingled with fears,
And the cup of thanksgiving with penitent tears:
The festival trump calls for jubilant songs,
But my spirit her own *miserere* prolongs.

I would not live always — no, welcome the tomb,
Since Jesus hath lain there I dread not its gloom;
Where he deigned to sleep, I'll too bow my head,
All peaceful to slumber on that hallowed bed.
Then the glorious daybreak, to follow that night,
The orient gleam of the angels of light,
With their clarion call for the sleepers to rise
And chant forth their matins, away to the skies.

Who, who would live always? Away from his God,
Away from yon heaven, that blissful abode,
Where the rivers of blessing flow over the bright plains,
And the noontide of glory eternally reigns;
Where the saints of all ages in harmony meet,
Their Savior and brethren transported to greet,
While the songs of salvation exultingly roll
And the smile of the Lord is the feast of the soul.

That heavenly music! What is it I hear?
The notes of the harpers ring sweet in mine ear!
And see soft, unfolding, those portals of gold,
The King all arrayed in his beauty behold!
Oh give me, oh give me, the wings of a dove,
To adore him — be near him — enwrapped with his love;
I but wait for the summons, I list for the word —
Alleluia — Amen — evermore with the Lord!

— *William Augustus Muhlenberg*

At left: The harshness of the Great Lakes region winter was certainly one reason for equipping this beautiful stone church with a tin roof. Note the octagonal, louvered steeple, and the rounded, Renaissance-style windows. *Above:* Built of stone, with a metal roof, but with a layout similar to that of its neighbor Coon Valley, Wisconsin church shown on page 82, this house of worship is surrounded by the faithful who have 'gone on before us.'

HAIL, QUEEN OF HEAVEN

Hail, Queen of heaven, the ocean star,
  Guide of the wanderer here below,
Thrown on life's surge, we claim thy care,
  Save us from peril and from woe.
Mother of Christ, Star of the sea,
  Pray for the wanderer, pray for me.

O gentle, chaste and spotless Maid,
  We sinners make our prayers through thee;
Remind thy Son that He has paid
  The price of our iniquity.
Virgin, most pure, Star of the sea,
  Pray for the sinner, pray for me.

Sojourners in this vale of tears,
  To thee, blest Advocate, we cry,
Pity our sorrows, calm our fears,
  And soothe with hope our misery.
Refuge in grief, Star of the sea,
  Pray for the mourner, pray for me.

And while to Him Who reigns above,
  In Godhead One, in Persons Three,
The Source of life, of grace, of love,
  Homage we pay on bended knee.
Do thou, bright Queen, Star of the sea,
  Pray for the children, pray for me.

—*Rev Dr Lingard*

Previous pages: The beautiful Cathedral on the Prairie in Hoven, South Dakota.
These pages: Scenes of Blue Cloud Abbey in Milbank, South Dakota. Mary is held
to be the Queen of heaven for her role in Christ's birth, and is a type of the church;
just so, church architecture mirrors the Kingdom of heaven.

THE TEMPLE OF THE PRAIRIE

Howl, you old winds,
but this house shall not be shaken,
for this is the house of God,
set down upon the flatlands
as a recompense, a reconciliation
and an admonishment
to the prairie winds
  'the Powers of the Air,'
that those who are sheltered here
are linked with invincible Might—
God's all-powerful Mercy.

— EM Duffield

At left: An enduring prairie church stands tall against the winds of the plains. *Above:* This country church in South Dakota bears, inscribed above its door, 'Koscial St Jozefa.' *Overleaf:* Union Point Church, in Manitoba.

RESTORATION OF A CHURCH

O Jerusalem the blissful, Home of gladness yet untold;
Thou whose countless throngs triumphal
fill with joy thy streets of gold;
Graven on thee, new and glorious,
they the King's own Name behold!

Many are thy sons, O Mother, yon august and shining band!
Gentle Peace in all thy borders
makes thee glad, O happy land!
Perfect is thy restoration, bright in holiness to stand.

Here, a figure of the Heavenly,
shines our temple, worthier grown
By its richer restoration on the old foundation-stone,
With a majesty and beauty to the former house unknown.

Lord, we pray Thee, Master Builder, Great and Holy, enter in,
Fill Thy sanctuary quickly, as our hallowing rites begin,
And Thyself its Consecrator rest for evermore therein.

Make, O Royal Priest, Thine Altar here
henceforth a Throne of light,
Ever held in highest honor, and with many a gift made bright,
Ever blessed, ever peaceful, ever precious in Thy sight.

Yea, our hearts, for these Thou judgest,
as Thy cleansed Altars bless,
By Thy Spirit's grace renew us unto perfect holiness,
And the sevenfold gifts from Heaven
grant us ever to possess.

— Anonymous

At left: A fine example of church restoration, 'The Little Brown Church in the Vale,' in Nashua, Iowa. Note the inscription on the step; see the song on page 63.
Above: Awaiting restoration — Holy Trinity Church, in Saskatchewan.

THE HOUSE IS NOT FOR ME

The house is not for me — it is for Him,
His royal thoughts require many a stair,
Many a tower, many an outlook fair
Of which I have no thought.

—*George MacDonald*

MATTHEW 8:8, 19 and 20

. . . Lord, I am not worthy that thou shouldest come under my roof . . . .

And a certain scribe came, and said unto him, Master, I will follow thee whithersoever thou goest.

And Jesus saith unto him, The foxes have holes, and the birds of the air have nests, but the Son of Man hath not where to lay his head.

Above left: It is a church that bears a similarity to many others—and, yet, despite outward appearances, the congregations of such as this edifice in Nebraska feel much more than its physical, Gothic-windowed presence in every aspect of their lives, wherever they are. *Above:* St Peter's Church, with its single spire raised in proclamation, and its faithful bell at the ready for ringing, exemplifies a missionary kind of structure, with its small chapel, and tiny, squared-off apse. Despite simplicity of construction, there is a graceful ambience to this structure. Its locale is Red Jacket, Saskatchewan.

THE SOUTHWEST

O SPIRIT OF THE LIVING GOD

O Spirit of the Living God!
  In all the fullness of Thy grace,
Wherever the foot of man hath trod,
  Descend on our apostate race.

Give tongues of fire and hearts of love
  To preach the reconciling word;
Give power and unction from above,
  Whenever the joyful sound is heard.

Be darkness, at Thy coming, light,
  Confusion order in Thy path;
Souls without strength inspire with might;
  Bid mercy triumph over wrath.

O Spirit of the Lord! Prepare
  All the round earth her God to meet;
Breathe Thou abroad like morning air,
  Till hearts of stone begin to beat.

Baptize the nations; far and nigh
  The triumphs of the Cross record;
The Name of Jesus glorify
  Till every kindred call Him Lord.

— Rev W Statham

Previous pages: From the missionary days of America's Old West — De Grazia's Mission, in Arizona. Native adobe allowed the missionaries to build sturdy structures that were proof against the fiery heat of the desert. *Above:* A Mission chapel at Lajitas, Texas, exhibiting a slab tower of the kind often built as a matter of expedience. *At right:* Native Americans of the Tigua tribe celebrate St Anthony's Day at historic Ysleta Mission in El Paso.

ACTS 2:17 – 18, 21, 38 – 42 and 46 – 47

And it shall come to pass in the last days, saith God, I will pour out of my Spirit upon all flesh: and your sons and your daughters shall prophesy, and your young men shall see visions, and your old men shall dream dreams . . .

And on my servants and on my handmaidens I will pour out in those days of my Spirit; and they shall prophesy . . .

And it shall come to pass, that whosoever shall call on the name of the Lord shall be saved.

Then Peter said unto them, Repent, and be baptized every one of you in the name of Jesus Christ for the remission of sins, and ye shall receive the gift of the Holy Ghost.

For the promise is unto you, and to your children, and to all that are afar off, even as many as the Lord our God shall call . . . .

Then they that gladly received his word were baptized: and the same day there were added unto them about three thousand souls.

And they continued steadfastly in the apostles' doctrine and fellowship, and in breaking of bread, and in prayers . . .

And they, continuing daily with one accord in the temple, and breaking bread from house to house, did eat their meat with gladness and singleness of heart.

Praising God, and having favor with all the people. And the Lord added to the church daily such as should be saved.

At left: San Jose de Gracia Church, in Las Trampas, New Mexico, with its twin towers and classic adobe structure, was built in the late 1700s. *Above:* San Miguel Mission, in Santa Fe, New Mexico, is the oldest church in the US. For a contrast, see Sacred Heart Church, in Galveston, Texas — on the *overleaf.*

THE CHURCH'S ONE FOUNDATION

The Church's one foundation
　is Jesus Christ her Lord;
She is his new creation
　By water and the word;
From heaven he came and sought her
　To be his holy bride;
With his own blood he bought her,
　And for her life he died.

Elect from every nation,
　Yet one o'er all the earth,
Her charter of salvation
　One Lord, one faith, one birth;
One holy name she blesses,
　Partakes one holy food,
And to one hope she presses,
　With every grace endowed.

'Mid toil and tribulation,
　And tumult of her war,
She waits the consummation
　Of peace forevermore;
Till with the vision glorious
　Her longing eyes are blest,
And the great Church victorious,
　Shall be the Church at rest.

Yet she on earth hath union
　With Father, Spirit, Son,
And mystic sweet communion
　With those whose rest is won;
O happy ones and holy;
　Lord, give us grace that we,
Like them, the meek and lowly,
　On high may dwell with Thee.

— Samuel J Stone

Above: Vereins Kirche, a Pioneer Memorial of the state of Texas, typifies the design of the octagonal church, a form that began in Classical times as the round temple, and in the Christian church is a form that signifies the one head, one foundation and one spirit of the church. *At right:* Salado Methodist Church, in Texas, has a nineteenth-century ambience, with its scalloped shingling and gabled steeple. A small wrought-iron lamp welcomes worshippers.

from
THE INDIAN

Many years ago, on the outskirts of a western settlement was a small homestead, which belonged to an industrious young farmer. At that time, the understanding between the whites and the Indians was not good. It was not often, however, that they came into the neighborhood of this homestead, though on one or two occasions a few Indians had been seen on the outskirts of the pine forest.

It was a lovely evening in June. The moon shed her silvery light all around, distinctly revealing every feature of the scene which has been described, and showed the tall, muscular figure of William Sullivan, who was seated upon the door steps, busily employed in preparing his scythes for the coming hay season. He was a good looking young fellow, with a sunburnt, open countenance; but though often kind hearted, he was filled with prejudices.

So intent was he upon his work, that he heeded not the approach of a tall Indian accoutered for a hunting excursion, until the words, 'Will you give a hunter some supper, and a lodging for the night?' in a tone of supplication, met his ear.

The young farmer raised his head; a look of contempt curling the corners of his mouth, and an angry gleam darting from his eyes, as he replied in a tone as uncourteous as his words, 'Heathen Indian dog, you shall have nothing here; begone!'

The Indian turned away; then again facing young Sullivan, he said in a pleading voice, 'I am hungry, it is long since I have eaten; give me a crust of bread and a bone to strengthen me.'

'Get you gone, heathen hound,' said the farmer, 'I have nothing for you.'

This was all that he could obtain from one who called himself a Christian, but who allowed prejudice and obstinacy to steel his heart.

continued on page 111

Above: Millard's Crossing Church at Nacogdoches, Texas, has a distinctive plainness that matches a heartfelt, simple and direct faith. *At right:* The beautifully simple La Lometa Mission, in Mission, Texas. Note the bell tower.

continued from page 108

The farmer's wife, Mary Sullivan, heard the whole as she sat hushing her infant to rest. Perceiving that her husband had finished his work, and was slowly bending his steps toward the stables with downcast eyes — for it must be confessed he did not feel very comfortable — she left the house, and was soon at the Indian's side, with a pitcher of milk in her hand, and a napkin, in which was a plentiful meal of bread and roasted kid, with a little parched corn as well.

'Will my red brother drink some milk?' said Mary, bending over the Indian; and as he arose to comply with her invitation, she untied the napkin and bade him eat and be refreshed.

When he had finished, the Indian said: 'I will protect the white dove from the pounces of the eagle; for her sake her red brother will not seek to be revenged.'

Drawing a bunch of heron's feathers from his bosom, he selected the longest, and giving it to Mary Sullivan, said, 'When the white dove's mate flies over the Indian's hunting-grounds, bid him wear this on his head.' He then turned away; and going into the woods, was soon lost to view.

The summer passed away; harvest had come and gone. Preparations now began to be made for a hunting excursion, and William Sullivan was included in the number who were going to try their fortune on the hunting-grounds beyond the river and the pine forests.

But now, as the time of their departure drew near, misgivings filled his mind, and his imagination was haunted by the form of the Indian, who in the preceding summer he had so harshly treated. On the eve of the day on which they were to start, he made known his anxiety to his gentle wife, confessing at the same time that his conscience had never ceased to reproach him for his unkind behavior; his conduct was displeasing in the sight of God, as well as cruel toward a suffering brother. Mary Sullivan heard her husband in silence. When he was done, she laid her hand in his, and told him what she had done, confessing at the same time that she had kept this to herself, fearing his displeasure. Going to a closet, she took out the beautiful heron's feather, repeating at the same time the parting words of the Indian.

'Nay,' said Sullivan, 'these Indians never forgive an injury.'

'Neither do they ever forget a kindness,' added Mary. 'I will sew this feather in your hunting cap, and then trust you, my own dear husband, to God's keeping. Now that my father is dead and gone, I think much more of what he used to say than when he was with me; and I fear that we are altogether wrong in the way we are going on, and I feel that if we were treated as we deserve, God would forget us, and leave us to ourselves, because we have so forgotten him.'

She was the only daughter of a pious English sailor, and in early girlhood had given promise of becoming all that a religious parent could desire. But her piety was then more of the head than of the heart, and like 'the morning cloud and the early dew,' her profession of religion vanished away, and she lost her relish for that in which she once had taken such delight. A long conversation followed; and that night saw the young couple kneeling for the first time in prayer at domestic worship.

The morning that witnessed the departure of the hunters was one of surpassing beauty. No cloud was to be seen upon the brow of William Sullivan. He put on his cap, shouldered his rifle, and the hunters were soon on their way seeking game.

William, in consequence of following a buck too ardently, separated from his companions, and in trying to rejoin them became bewildered. Hour after hour he sought in vain for some mark by which he might thread the intricacy of the forest, and not being much accustomed to the woodman's life, he could not find his way.

Toward sunset the trees lessened and grew thinner, and by and by he found himself upon the outskirts of an immense prairie. A river ran not far off, and toward it, Sullivan directed his lagging footsteps. He had not eaten anything since the morning. A rustling in the underwood made him pause, and the next instant out rushed an enormous buffalo. The buffalo paused for a moment, and then lowering his enormous head, rushed forward toward the intruder.

It knocked him to the ground, preparing to trample him to death, when he heard the sharp crack of a rifle behind him, and in another instant the animal fell heavily close by the prostrate Sullivan. A dark form in Indian garb glided by a moment after, and plunged his hunting-knife deep into the neck of the buffalo, so as to bleed the animal, thus to render the flesh more suitable for keeping a greater length of time.

The Indian then turned to Sullivan. 'If the weary hunter will rest till morning, the eagle will show him the way to the nest of his white dove,' he said. Then taking him by the hand, he led him through the rapidly increasing darkness, until they reached a small encampment lying near the river. Here the Indian gave Sullivan a plentiful supply of hominy and some venison; then spreading some skins of animals for his bed, he signed to him to occupy it, and left him to his repose.

The light of dawn had not yet appeared in the east when the Indian awoke Sullivan; and after a slight repast, they started for the settlement of the whites. The Indian threaded his way through the still-darkened forest far more quickly than Sullivan had done, and before the golden sun had sunk behind the summits of the far-off mountains, Sullivan once more stood within view of his beloved home. Turning toward the Indian, he poured forth his heartfelt thanks for the service he had rendered him.

The warrior, who till then had not allowed his face to be seen by Sullivan, except in the imperfect light of his

continued on page 112

At left: A kindly friar addresses a pair of young Native American parishioners in front of the beautiful bas-relief facade (typical of the Southwestern Spanish influence) of San Xavier del Bac, in Tucson, Arizona. *Above:* Another view of San Xavier, showing towers with ornate buttresses and balustrades.

continued from page 111

wigwam, now fronted him, allowing the sun's rays to fall upon his person, and revealed to the astonished young man the features of the very same Indian whom, five months before, he had so cruelly repulsed. His voice was gentle and low as he said: 'Five moons ago, when I was faint and weary, you called me "Indian dog," and drove me from your door. I might last night have been revenged; but the white dove fed me, and for her sake I spared her mate. I bid you to go home, and when hereafter you see a red man in need of kindness, do to him as you have been done to.'

Sullivan so earnestly entreated him to go with him, as a proof that he had indeed forgiven his brutal treatment, that he at last consented, and the humbled farmer led him to his cottage. There his wife's surprise at seeing him so soon was only equaled by her thankfulness at his wonderful escape from danger and by her gratitude to the man who had thus repaid her act of kindness, forgetful of the provocation he had received from her husband.

Many were the visits the Indian paid to the cottage of the once prejudiced and churlish Sullivan, who now was no longer so — for the practical lesson of kindness he had learned was not lost upon him. It was made the means of bringing William Sullivan to a knowledge of his own sinfulness in the sight of God, and his deficiencies in duty toward his fellow men.

The Indian's kindness was repaid to him indeed a hundredfold. At length it pleased the Lord to bless the unwearied teaching of his white friends to his spiritual good, and to give an answer to the prayer of faith. The Indian was the first native convert baptized by the American missionary, who came about two years after to a station some few miles distant from the Sullivan's cottage. The warrior — who once had wielded the tomahawk in mortal strife against both whites and Indians — went forth, armed with a far different weapon, 'even the sword of the Spirit, which is the word of God,' to make known to his countrymen 'the glad tidings of great joy' that 'Christ Jesus came into the world to save sinners,' whether they be bond or free, white or red, for 'we are all one in Christ.' Many years he thus labored, until, worn out with toil and age, he returned to his white friends' home, where in a few months he fell asleep in Jesus, giving to his friends the certain hope of a joyful meeting hereafter at the resurrection of the just.

Many years have passed since then. There is no trace now of the cottage of the Sullivans — who both rest in the same forest churchyard where lie the bones of their good friend — but their descendants still dwell in the same township. Often does the gray-haired grandpa tell this little history to his grandchildren, while seated under the stately magnolia which shades the graves of the quiet sleepers of whom he speaks. And the lesson which he teaches to his youthful hearers, is 'Whatsoever ye would that men should do to you, do ye even so to them.'

— *MA Vroman*

The altar (*above*) of La Villita Church, in San Antonio, Texas. The stained glass window is a mosaic radiant cross — a very ancient, yet timeless, motif. *At right:* The ornate, Spanish-style San Jose Mission in San Antonio, Texas.

WEST

AMAZING GRACE

Amazing grace! How sweet the sound,
   That saved a wretch like me!
I once was lost, but now am found,
   Was blind, but now I see.

'Twas grace that taught my heart to fear,
   And grace my fears relieved;
How precious did that grace appear
   The hour I first believed!

Through many dangers, toils and snares,
   I have already come;
'Tis grace hath brought me safe thus far,
   And grace will lead me home.

When we've been there ten thousand years,
   Bright shining as the sun,
We've no less days to sing God's praise
   Than when we first begun.

— John Newton

Previous pages: The extremely modern US Air Force Academy Chapel, near Colorado Springs, Colorado. *Above right and right:* The Church of Jesus Christ of Latter-Day Saints Tabernacle in Jordan River, Utah, shows a Mormon mode of emphasizing the heavenward sweep of walls and towers with pillars, pilasters and other vertical motifs — compare with St Elizabeth's Catholic Church *(above),* in Denver; built in 1896, with renovations in the 1930s and 1960s.

YOUR HOUSE

Your house is in the city;
your house is in the country.
In the wilderness, where peaks
    are far pavilions, and where
    the little grasses and tall trees
    rise up from the earth,
Your house rose likewise, years ago,
    from mountain stone.
In the busy streets of town,
    where the work of
    man's hands and his automobiles
    give prominent voice to the spirit
    of 'city,'
Your house stands strong,
    foursquare, giving voice to those
    whose ears can hear,
    whose hearts yearn like the grass
    toward the sun of your Word.

— *Andrew Jacobs*

Above: First Baptist Church of Missoula, Montana. Note the mortise-and-tenon parapet above the entryway, which gives the truncated tower the appearance of a castle wall, or a king's crown. *At right:* A rustic stone chapel in Colorado.

from
GOD'S TEMPLES

Blest are the country churches!
  I love their simple ways,
Their heartfelt hymns, that clearly
Soar up to God sincerely;
My heart remembers dearly
  Those bygone Sabbath days.

No carven pulpits gleaming,
  No wide and stately halls,
No brass and silver railing,
  Just shady porches, dreaming,
  And graceful ivy, trailing
  Over the time-stained walls.

I sought God in cathedrals
  Vast aisles of white and gold;
Where waves of glorious music
  From the great organ rolled.
But God seemed high in Heaven.
  I could not sense Him there;
In all the pomp and glory
  There seemed no room for prayer.

Ah, give me little churches
  My happy childhood knew!
Time-hallowed, gentle places,
Hid among elms and birches,
Dear little country churches —
  I think God loves them, too!

— *Edith D Osborne*

Above: Alberta's Markerville Lutheran Church — with leaded, Gothic windows up front and plain rectangles on the sides — was built in 1907. *At left:* St Paul's Episcopal Church, which was moved from Aspen to Marble, Colorado, in 1909.

PSALM 98

O sing unto the Lord a new song; for he hath done marvelous things: his right hand, and his holy arm, hath gotten him the victory.

The Lord hath made known his salvation: his righteousness hath he openly showed in the sight of the heathen.

He hath remembered his mercy and his truth toward the house of Israel: all the ends of the earth have seen the salvation of our God.

Make a joyful noise unto the Lord, all the earth: make a loud noise, and rejoice, and sing praise.

Sing unto the Lord with the harp; with the harp, and the voice of a psalm.

With trumpets and sound of cornet make a joyful noise before the Lord, the King.

Let the sea roar, and the fullness thereof; the world, and they that dwell therein.

Let the floods clap their hands: let the hills be joyful together

Before the Lord; for he cometh to judge the earth; with righteousness shall he judge the world, and the people with equity.

Stained glass Annunciation, and celebration. *Above:* With the dove of the Holy Spirit shedding grace upon the scene, the Angel Gabriel announces to Mary that she will bear the Christ child. *At right:* Angels make joyous music to the glory of God. *Overleaf:* Twin-towered St Cajetan's Church, in Denver, Colorado.

WAITING FOR THE COMING OF OUR LORD JESUS CHRIST

Lord, her watch Thy Church is keeping;
   When shall earth Thy rule obey?
When shall end the night of weeping?
   When shall break the promised day?
See the whitening harvest languish,
   Waiting still the laborer's toil;
Was it in vain, Thy Son's deep anguish?
   Shall the strong retain the spoil?

Tidings, sent to every creature,
   Millions yet have never heard;
Can they hear without a preacher?
   Lord Almighty, give the Word:
Give the Word; in every nation
   Let the Gospel trumpet sound,
Witnessing a world's salvation
   To the earth's remotest bound.

Then the end: Thy Church completed,
   All Thy chosen gathered in,
With their King in Glory seated,
   Satan bound, and banished sin;
Gone forever parting, weeping,
   Hunger, sorrow, death and pain;
Lo! her watch Thy Church is keeping;
   Come, Lord Jesus, come to reign.

— Henry Smart

JOHN 10:1 – 6

Verily, verily, I say unto you, He that entereth not by the door into the sheepfold, but climbeth up some other way, the same is a thief and a robber.

But he that entereth in by the door is the shepherd of the sheep.

To him the porter openeth; and the sheep hear his voice: and he calleth his own sheep by name, and leadeth them out.

And when he putteth forth his own sheep, he goeth before them, and the sheep follow him: for they know his voice.

And a stranger will they not follow, but will flee from him: for they know not the voice of strangers.

This parable spake Jesus unto them: but they understood not what things they were which he spake unto them.

At right: The Sheldon Jackson Memorial Chapel in Fairplay, Colorado, was dedicated in 1874. A very elegant Victorian structure, it stands as a landmark of another era for Presbyterians in the Mountain West of the US.

JESUS, WHERE'ER THY PEOPLE MEET

Jesus, where'er Thy people meet,
　There they behold Thy mercy-seat;
Where'er they seek Thee Thou art found,
　And every place is hallowed ground.

For Thou, within no walls confined,
　Inhabitest the humble mind;
Such ever bring Thee when they come,
　And going, take Thee to their home.

Great Shepherd of Thy chosen few,
　Thy former mercies here renew;
Here to our waiting hearts proclaim
　The sweetness of Thy saving Name.

Here may we prove the power of prayer,
　To strengthen faith and sweeten care,
To teach our faint desires to rise,
　And bring all Heaven before our eyes.

Lord, we are few, but Thou are near,
　Nor short Thine arm, nor deaf Thine ear;
O rend the Heavens, come quickly down,
　And make a thousand hearts Thine own.

—*William Cowper*

Above: Central to Central City, Colorado are these two churches, located right around the hillside from one another. The nearer church is a cruciform building, with a hip-roofed tower; one of its transepts is visible to us on its right; the other church is a box structure with a truncated tower reminiscent of Reformation structures. *At right:* Another view of the Sheldon Jackson Memorial Chapel. Note the rosette decoration, and the operable bell.

from
APPRECIATION AND CRITICISMS OF THE WORK OF CHARLES DICKENS

I heard that in some debating clubs there is a rule that the members may discuss anything except religion and politics. I cannot imagine what they do discuss; but it is quite evident that they have ruled out the only two subjects which are either important or amusing. The thing is a part of a certain modern tendency to avoid things because they lead to warmth; whereas, obviously, we ought, even in a social sense, to seek those things specially. The warmth of the discussion is as much a part of hospitality as the warmth of the fire. And it is singularly suggestive that in English literature the two things have died together. The very people who would blame Dickens for his sentimental hospitality are the very people who would also blame him for his narrow political conviction. The very people who would mock him for his narrow radicalism are those who would mock him for his broad fireside. Real conviction and real charity are much nearer than people suppose. Dickens was capable of loving all men; but he refused to love all opinions. The modern humanitarian can love all opinions, but he cannot love all men; he seems, sometimes, in the ecstasy of his humanitarianism, even to hate them all. He can love all opinions, including the opinion that men are unlovable.

— GK Chesterton

REMEMBER, HOLY MARY

Remember, holy Mary,
  'Twas never heard or known
That any one who sought thee
  And made to thee his moan,
That any one who hastened
  For shelter to thy care,
Was ever yet abandoned
  And left to his despair.

And so to thee, my Mother,
  With filial faith I call,
For Jesus dying gave thee
  As Mother to us all.
To thee, O Queen of virgins,
  O Mother meek, to thee
I run with trustful fondness,
  Like child to mother's knee.

See at thy feet a sinner,
  Groaning and weeping sore —
Ah! throw thy mantle o'er me,
  And let me stray no more.
Thy Son has died to save me,
  And from His throne on high
His Heart this moment yearneth
  For even such as I.

All, all His love remember,
  And, oh! Remember too
How prompt I am to purpose,
  How slow and frail to do.
Yet scorn not my petitions,
  but patiently give ear,
And help me, O my Mother,
  Most loving and most dear.

—from a Slovak hymnal

At right: This Ukrainian Orthodox Church in Edmonton, Alberta, is a cruciform, octagonal church, with octagonal nave; half-octagonal apse and transepts; and rectangular narthex. The five onion domes atop this church symbolize Christ and the four Evangelists. The Orthodox Church is often depicted as under the protective influence of Mary, the mother of all Christians. *Overleaf:* Our Lady of Guadalupe Church, Colorado's oldest, in Conejos.

THE MASTER'S HAND

In the still air the music lies unheard;
   In the rough marble beauty hides unseen;
To make the music and the beauty needs
   A master's touch, the sculptor's chisel keen.

Great Master, touch us with Thy skilled hand:
   Let not the music that is in us die!
Great Sculptor, hew and polish us, nor let
   Hidden and lost, Thy form within us lie!

Spare not the stroke! Do with us as thou wilt!
   Let aught be broken, healed and scored;
Complete Thy purpose, that we may become
   Thy perfect image, Thou our God and Lord.

—MA Vroman

At left: Denver's Basilica of the Immaculate Conception. The basilican plan originated in the Roman public hall, which was rectangular, with a nave — that was divided into two aisles by columnades — and an apse, behind the altar of which sat the judges or officials. Such courts of law were easily taken as practical and symbolic bases for Christian churches — with the 'Righteous and Merciful Judge' presiding. *Above:* Boise Valley Baptist Church, Idaho.

JOHN 3:31 – 36

He that cometh from above is above all; he that is of the earth is earthly, and speaketh of the earth: he that cometh from heaven is above all.

And what he hath seen and heard, that he testifieth; and no man receiveth his testimony.

He that hath received his testimony hath set to his seal that God is true.

For he whom God hath sent speaketh the words of God: for God giveth not the Spirit by measure unto him.

The Father loveth the Son, and hath given all things into his hand.

He that believeth on the Son hath everlasting life . . .

from
THE FIRST MEETING

And all the time it was God near her that was making her unhappy. For as the Son of Man came not to send peace on the earth but a sword, so the first visit of God to the human soul is generally in a cloud of fear and doubt, rising from the soul itself at His approach. The sun is the cloud dispeller, yet often he must look through a fog if he would visit the earth at all.

— *George MacDonald*

At right: Historic St Mary's Mission, in Montana's rugged Rocky Mountains. The growth, and success of this mission can be estimated by the incremental additions — denoted by the major seams along its side — seen here.

PSALM 132:4–16

I will not give sleep to mine eyes or slumber to mine eyelids,

Until I find out a place for the Lord, a habitation for the mighty God of Jacob.

Lo, we heard of it at Ephratah: we found it in the fields of the wood.

We will go into his tabernacles: we will worship at his footstool.

Arise, O Lord, into thy rest: thou, and the ark of thy strength.

Let thy priests be clothed with righteousness; and let thy saints shout for joy.

For thy servant David's sake turn not away the face of thine anointed.

The Lord hath sworn in truth unto David; he will not turn from it. Of the fruit of thy body will I set upon thy throne.

If thy children will keep my covenant and my testimony that I shall teach them, their children shall also sit upon thy throne for evermore.

For the Lord hath chosen Zion; he hath desired it for his habitation.

This is my rest forever: here will I dwell; for I have desired it.

I will abundantly bless her provision: I will satisfy her poor with bread.

I will also clothe her priests with salvation: and her saints shall shout aloud for joy.

Previous pages: A cruciform Russian Orthodox church in Unalaska, Alaska. *At right* is an octagonal Russian Orthodox church in Juneau. Note the bell tower over the narthex. Orthodox cross symbology—the bar at the bottom slants to differentiate the repentant and the unrepentant thieves, the middle bar is for Christ's sacrifice; the top bar is the proclamation of Christ as King. *Above:* Sacred statuary —a Roman Catholic practice—and a stone church in Juneau.

EPHESIANS 5:25-33

Husbands, love your wives, even as Christ also loved the church, and gave himself for it;

That he might sanctify and cleanse it with the washing of water by the word,

That he might present it to himself a glorious church, not having spot, or wrinkle, or any such thing; but that it should be holy and without blemish.

So ought men to love their wives as their own bodies. He that loveth his wife loveth himself.

For no man ever yet hated his own flesh; but nourisheth and cherisheth it, even as the Lord the church:

For we are members of his body, of his flesh, and of his bones.

For this cause shall a man leave his father and mother, and shall be joined unto his wife; and they two shall be one flesh.

This is a great mystery: but I speak concerning Christ and the church.

Nevertheless let every one of you in particular so love his wife even as himself; and the wife see that she reverence her husband.

Above: The bars on the Orthodox cross (see caption, previous page), also symbolize — hell, this world and heaven. *At right:* A cruciform Orthodox church in Kodiak. Note the icon — an Orthodox practice — above the entrance.

I TIMOTHY 3:14–16

These things write I unto thee, hoping to come unto thee shortly:

But if I tarry long, that thou mayest know how thou oughtest to behave thyself in the house of God, which is the church of the living God, the pillar and ground of the truth.

And without controversy great is the mystery of godliness: God was manifest in the flesh, justified in the Spirit, seen of angels, preached unto the Gentiles, believed on in the world, received up into glory.

At left: Greenery and twin gables — St Philip's Episcopal Church in Wrangell, Alaska, is much like a manor house for respected guests. *Above:* A stone church in Skagway. *At right:* A mission church in Fort Good Hope, Northwest Territories.

HAGGAI 2:3-9

Who is left among you that saw this house in her first glory? And how do ye see it now? Is it not in your eyes in comparison of it as nothing?

Yet now be strong, O Zerubbabel, saith the Lord; and be strong, O Joshua, son of Josedech, the high priest; and be strong, all ye people of the land, saith the Lord, and work: for I am with you, saith the Lord of hosts:

According to the word that I covenanted with you when ye came out of Egypt, so my spirit remaineth among you: fear ye not.

For thus saith the Lord of hosts; Yet once, it is a little while, and I will shake the heavens, and the earth, and the sea and the dry land;

And I will shake all nations, and the desire of all nations shall come: and I will fill this house with glory, saith the Lord of hosts.

The silver is mine, and the gold is mine, saith the Lord of hosts.

The glory of this latter house shall be greater than of the former, saith the Lord of hosts: and in this place will I give peace, saith the Lord of hosts.

At left: The interior and iconostasis of the Orthodox church *above*, in Alaska's Pribilof Islands. On the near stand is an icon of the eighteenth century priestmonk, St Herman, who led the Aleuts to the faith and succored them in their, and his own, persecution. *At right:* An unusual Orthodox church in Sitka.

COAST

PROTESTANT CHURCH

FESTIVAL OF THE
DEDICATION OF A CHURCH

'I, John, saw the holy city, new Jerusalem, coming down
from God out of heaven, prepared as a bride adorned for her
husband.'

Blessed city, heavenly Salem,
  Vision dear of peace and love,
Who of living stones art builded
  In the height of heaven above,
And, with Angel hosts encircled,
  As a bride dost earthward move;

From celestial realms descending,
  Bridal glory round thee shed,
Meet for Him Whose love espoused thee,
  To thy Lord shalt thou be led;
All thy streets, and all thy bulwarks
  Of pure gold are fashioned.

Bright thy gates of pearl are shining,
  They are open evermore;
And by virtue of His merits
  Thither faithful souls do soar,
Who for Christ's dear Name in this world
  Pain and tribulation bore.

Many a blow and biting sculpture
  Polished well those stones elect,
In their places now compacted
  By the heavenly Architect,
Who therewith hath willed forever
  That His Palace should be decked.

Christ is made the sure Foundation,
  Christ the Head and Cornerstone,
Chosen of the Lord, and precious,
  Binding all the Church in one,
Holy Zion's help forever,
  And her confidence alone.

All that dedicated city,
  Dearly loved of God on high,
In exultant jubilation
  Pours perpetual melody,
God the One in Three adoring
  In glad hymns eternally.

To this Temple, where we call Thee,
  Come, O Lord of hosts, today;
With Thy wonted loving kindness
  Hear Thy servants, as they pray;
And Thy fullest benediction
  Shed within its wall always.

Here vouchsafe to all Thy servants
  What they ask of Thee to gain,
What they gain from Thee forever
  With the Blessed to retain,
And hereafter in Thy glory
  Evermore with Thee to reign.

Laud and honor to the Father,
  Laud and honor to the Son,
Laud and honor to the Spirit,
  Ever Three, and ever One,
Consubstantial, Co-eternal
  While unending ages run.

—Rev JM Neale, translator

REVEALED TO BABES

The wise and prudent must make a system and arrange things to his mind before he can say, *I believe*. The child sees, believes, obeys — and knows he must be perfect as his Father in heaven is perfect. If an angel, seeming to come from heaven, told him that God had let him off, that He did not require so much of him, but would be content with less . . . the child would at once recognize, woven with the angel's starry brillancy, the flicker of flames . . . .

Christ is the way out, and the way in: the way from slavery, conscious or unconscious, into liberty; the way from the unhomeliness of things to the home we desire but do not know; the way from the stormy skirts of the Father's garments to the peace of His bosom.

— George MacDonald

Above: A welcoming and admonitory sign fronts the contemporary-style First Christian Church in Bellflower, California. A neighborly distance down Clark Avenue is Calvary Baptist Church *(at right)*, with its neo-classical portico and pediment — which, as do the triple doors, signifies the Trinity.

THE WORD, DESCENDING
FROM ABOVE

The Word, descending from above,
   Though with the Father still on high,
Went forth upon His work of love,
   And soon to life's last eve drew nigh.

He shortly to a death accursed
   By a disciple false was given
But, to His twelve disciples,
   First He gave Himself, the Bread from Heaven.

O Saving sacrifice! Open wide
   The gate of Heaven to man below!
Sore press our foes from every side;
   Thine aid supply, Thy strength bestow.

At birth our Brother He became;
   At meat Himself as food He gives;
To ransom us He died in shame;
   As our reward, in bliss He lives.

To Thy great Name be endless praise,
   Immortal Godhead, One in Three!
Oh, grant us endless length of days,
   In our true native land, with Thee!

—Rev E Caswall

At left: The Church of the Blessed Sacrament, in Hollywood, California, with renovation in progress on its tower. Images of St Thomas and St Clare occupy niches on the facade, and above the mullioned window is the Jesuit motto, which means 'To the Greater Glory of God.' *Above left:* The entry doors bear a wheat-sheaf motif, symbolic of the bread that is part of the Communion Sacrament. *Above:* The modern church signboard in aluminum and glass.

from
THE PRIEST OF SPRING

The sun has strengthened and the air softened just before Easter Day. But it is a troubled brightness which has a breath not only of novelty but of revolution. There are two great armies of the human intellect who will fight till the end on this vital point, whether Easter is to be congratulated on fitting in with the spring — or the spring on fitting in with Easter.

Now it is this simple truth which, like many others, is too simple for our scientists to see. This is where they go wrong, not only about true religion, but about false religions too; so that their account of mythology is more mythical than the myth itself.

There is one piece of nonsense that modern people still find themselves saying, even after they are more or less awake, by which I am particularly irritated. The fragment of gibberish to which I refer generally takes the form of saying: 'This god or hero really represents the sun.' Or: 'The King dying in a western battle is a *symbol* of the sun setting in the west.' Now I should really have thought that even the skeptical professors, whose skulls are as shallow as frying-pans, might have reflected that human beings never think or feel like this.

Quite plainly, of course, the case is just the other way. The god was never a symbol or hieroglyph representing the sun. The sun was a hieroglyph representing the god. We human beings have never worshipped Nature; and indeed, the reason is very simple. It is that all human beings are superhuman beings. We have printed our own image upon Nature, as God has printed His image upon us. We have told the enormous sun to stand still; we have fixed him on our shields, caring no more for a star than for a starfish.

About all these myths my own position is utterly and even sadly simple. I say you cannot really understand any myths till you have found that one of them is *not* a myth. Forged bank notes mean nothing if there are no real bank notes. Heathen gods mean nothing, and must always mean nothing, to those of us that deny the Christian God. When once a god is admitted, even a false god, the Cosmos begins to know its place: which is the second place. When once it is the real God, the Cosmos falls down before Him, offering flowers in spring as flames in winter. 'Christ is the Sun of Easter' does not mean that the worshiper is praising the sun under the emblem of Christ. And when I look across the fields, I know in my inmost bones that my joy is not solely in the spring; for spring alone, being always returning, would be always sad. There is somebody or something walking there, to be crowned with flowers: and my pleasure is in some promise yet possible and in the resurrection of the dead.

— *GK Chesterton*

These pages: Weathered and historic St Ann's Chapel, situated on the O'Keefe Ranch in Vernon, British Columbia. Its sun-bleached boards and ancient styling remind the visitor that The Priest of Spring can manifest His miracles of renewal even in such rustic surroundings. Many a prayer has been said here, and many a prayer has been answered. Note the plain cross, rose window with cruciform tracery, and pointed, Gothic, window above the door.

158

THE FIRST AND PRESENT CHRISTIANS

They went into the wilderness
    to seek the Lord, away
from those who would distract them,
suffering death by wild beasts,
starvation and exposure
    in their desire for prayer,
    for the quietude of that
    'still, small voice.'

Centuries passed, and those
    whose sufferings these were,
had built a sacred vessel — the center
    of the church —
with their pure monastic labors.

They have always led the way,
    so that others might come
to call men *out* of the
    spiritual wilderness.

— *Andrew Jacobs*

Above: A view through the portico at the central courtyard of a California mission, once part of El Camino Real, the Royal Road, on which the missions were spaced one day's travel apart. *At right:* The emblem of Christian life.

PSALM 90:1 – 4, 10 and 12 – 17

Lord, thou hast been our dwelling place in all generations.

Before the mountains were brought forth, or ever thou hadst formed the earth and the world, even from everlasting to everlasting, thou art God.

Thou turnest man to destruction; and sayest, 'Return, ye children of men.'

For a thousand years in thy sight are but as yesterday when it is past, and as a watch in the night . . .

The days of our years are threescore years and ten; and if by reason of strength they be fourscore years, yet is their strength labor and sorrow; for it is soon cut off, and we fly away . . .

So teach us to number our days, that we may apply our hearts unto wisdom.

Return, O Lord, how long? And let it repent thee concerning thy servants.

O satisfy us early with thy mercy; that we may rejoice and be glad all our days.

Make us glad according to the days wherein thou hast afflicted us, and the year wherein we have seen evil.

Let thy work appear unto thy servants, and thy glory unto their children.

And let the beauty of the Lord our God be upon us; and establish thou the work of our hands upon us; yea, the work of our hands establish thou it.

Above: A redwood-shingled chapel with a mansard roof. Note the ornamental buttresses under the eaves, and the Gothic doorway. *At right:* An abandoned California church. Many of the Gold Rush camps and towns sprang up, had a few years of prosperity, and then fell upon hard times. Besides the usual hard drinkers and gamblers, there were those miners and other men and women who felt an urge toward the spiritual—hence, churches like this were built.

PSALM 27:1 – 6

The Lord is my light and my salvation; whom shall I fear? The Lord is the strength of my life; of whom shall I be afraid?

When the wicked, even mine enemies and my foes, came upon me to eat up my flesh, they stumbled and fell.

Though an host should encamp against me, my heart shall not fear; though war should rise against me, in this will I be confident.

One thing have I desired of the Lord, that will I seek after: that I may dwell in the house of the Lord all the days of my life, to behold the beauty of the Lord, and to inquire in his temple.

For in the time of trouble he shall hide me in his pavilion; in the secret of his tabernacle shall he hide me; he shall set me up upon a rock.

And now shall mine head be lifted up above mine enemies round about me: therefore will I offer to his tabernacle sacrifices of joy; I will sing, yea, I will sing praises unto the Lord.

The first Catholic Church in Downieville was built in 1852. It was destroyed by fire in 1858, and was replaced that same year with the structure shown *at left*, which is still in use. Note the extreme simplicity of its design, with its tower over the entrance, and a meeting-hall style nave stretching out behind to the rectory. *Above:* This rustic chapel is situated across the road from the cemetery in historic Gold Rush-era Fiddletown, California.

FAITH OF OUR FATHERS

Faith of our fathers! Living still
  In spite of dungeon, fire and sword;
Oh, how our hearts beat high with joy
  Whenever we hear that glorious word.

Our fathers, chained in prisons dark,
  Were still in heart and conscience free:
How sweet would be their children's fate,
  If they, like them, could die for thee!

Faith of our fathers! We will love
  Both friend and foe in all our strife:
And preach thee too, as love knows how
  By kindly words and virtuous life.

— Father Faber

Above: The chapel at Fort Ross, the historic Russian fur traders' fort in Northern California. The Russians crossed the Bering Strait, and their Orthodox monks and priests spread the faith in the Far North. They came down the western coastline from Alaska, which was Russian territory until 1867. This California landmark is extremely well-preserved, complete with icons. *At right:* The historic Church of the Holy Cross in Skookumchuk, British Columbia.

PSALM 116

I love the Lord, because he hath heard my voice and my supplications.

Because he hath inclined his ear unto me, therefore will I call upon him as long as I live.

The sorrows of death compassed me, and the pains of hell got hold upon me: I found trouble and sorrow.

Then called I upon the name of the Lord; O Lord, I beseech thee, deliver my soul.

Gracious is the Lord, and righteous; yea, our God is merciful.

The Lord preserveth the simple: I was brought low, and he helped me.

Return unto thy rest, O my soul; for the Lord hath dealt bountifully with thee.

For thou has delivered my soul from death, mine eyes from tears, and my feet from falling.

I will walk before the Lord in the land of the living.

I believed, therefore have I spoken: I was greatly afflicted: I said in my haste, All men are liars.

What shall I render unto the Lord for all his benefits toward me?

I will take the cup of salvation, and call upon the name of the Lord.

I will pay my vows unto the Lord now in the presence of all his people.

Precious in the sight of the Lord is the death of his saints.

O Lord, truly I am thy servant; and the son of thine handmaid: thou has loosed my bonds.

I will offer to thee the sacrifice of thanksgiving, and will call upon the name of the Lord.

I will pay my vows unto the Lord now in the presence of all his people,

In the courts of the Lord's house, in the midst of thee, O Jerusalem. Praise ye the Lord.

At left: San Juan Capistrano Mission Catholic Church (see also, pages 168 – 169). *Above right:* A votive image of Father Junipero Serra, the missionary of 'The Royal Road' (see page 158), of which this mission was the first. *Above left:*

A Mary shrine at the mission, with an image of the Mother of Jesus Christ in a stance offering her protective mantle to all Christians. The mystic presence of the Holy Spirit is represented by the doves seen here.

AS FADES THE GLOWING ORB OF DAY

As fades the glowing orb of day,
  To Thee, great source of light, we pray;
Blest Three in One, to every heart
  Thy beams of life and love impart.

At early dawn, at close of day,
  To Thee our vows we humbly pay;
May we amid joys that never end,
  With Thy bright saints in homage bend.

— *TJ Potter, translator*

At left: A plaque at San Juan Capistrano Mission Church. *Above:* A side chapel of the church. *At right:* A bell like those that peal devotional hours and proclaim births and deaths. *Overleaf:* St Paul's Church, in North Vancouver, BC.

I KINGS 6:1–7
and JOHN 10:7–11, 22–23

And it came to pass in the four hundred and eightieth year after the children of Israel were come out of the land of Egypt, in the fourth year of Solomon's reign over Israel, in the month Zif, which is the second month, that he began to build the house of the Lord.

And the house which kind Solomon built for the Lord, the length thereof was threescore cubits, and the breadth thereof twenty cubits and the height thereof thirty cubits.

And the porch before the temple of the house, twenty cubits was the length thereof, according to the breadth of the house; and ten cubits was the breadth thereof before the house.

And for the house he made windows of narrow lights.

And against the wall of the house he built chambers round about, against the walls of the house round about, both of the temple and of the oracle: and he made chambers round about:

The nethermost chamber was five cubits broad, and the middle was six cubits broad, and the third was seven cubits broad: for without in the walls of the house he made narrowed rests round about, that the beams should not be fastened in the walls of the house.

And the house, when it was in building, was built of stone made ready before it was brought thither: so that there was neither hammer nor axe nor any tool of iron heard in the house, while it was in building.

. . . Then said Jesus unto them again Verily, verily, I say unto you: I am the door of the sheep.

All that ever came before me are thieves and robbers: but the sheep did not hear them.

I am the door: by me if any man enter in, he shall be saved, and shall go in and out, and find pasture.

The thief cometh not but for to steal, and to kill, and to destroy: I am come that they might have life, and that they might have it more abundantly.

I am the good shepherd: the good shepherd giveth his life for the sheep.

. . . And it was at Jerusalem the feast of the dedication, and it was winter.

And Jesus walked in the temple in Solomon's porch . . . .

At right: St Paul's Church (see also pages 170–171), a wooden cruciform structure in the Gothic mode. *At left:* The roseate cross—the fragrant gift of communion; new life in the resurrection; and thorn of beatific humility.

LOVE DIVINE

Love Divine, all loves excelling,
    Joy of Heaven, to earth come down,
Fix in us Thy humble dwelling,
    All Thy faithful mercies crown.

Jesus, Thou art all compassion,
    Pure unbounded love Thou art;
Visit us with Thy salvation,
    Enter every trembling heart.

Come Almighty to deliver,
    Let us all Thy grace receive;
Suddenly return, and never,
    Nevermore Thy temples leave.

Thee we would be always blessing,
    Serve Thee as Thy Hosts above;
Pray, and praise Thee, without ceasing,
    Glory in Thy perfect love.

Finish then Thy new creation,
    Pure and spotless let us be;
Let us see Thy great salvation,
    Perfectly restored in Thee.

Changed from glory into glory,
    Till in Heaven we take our place,
Till we cast our crowns before Thee,
    Lost in wonder, love and praise.

—Rev C Wesley

At right: With its heraldic, botonee ('knobbed,' or 'buttoned') cross atop its simple, louvered steeple, Santa Barbara Church in Randsburg, California is a humble yet archetypal image of the North American country church.

MICAH 4:1–8

But in the last days it shall come to pass, that the mountain of the house of the Lord shall be established in the top of the mountains, and it shall be exalted above the hills; and people shall flow unto it.

And many nations shall come, and say, Come, and let us go up to the mountain of the Lord, and to the house of the God of Jacob; and he will teach us of his ways, and we will walk in his paths: for the law shall go forth of Zion, and the word of the Lord from Jerusalem.

And he shall judge among many people, and rebuke strong nations afar off; and they shall beat their swords into plowshares, and their spears into pruninghooks: nation shall not lift up a sword against nation, neither shall they learn war any more.

But they shall sit every man under his vine and under his fig tree; and none shall make them afraid: for the mouth of the Lord of hosts, hath spoken it.

For all people will walk every one in the name of his god, and we will walk in the name of the Lord our God forever and ever.

In that day, saith the Lord, will I assemble her that halteth, and I will gather her that is driven out, and her that I have afflicted;

And I will make her that halted a remnant, and her that was cast far off a strong nation: and the Lord shall reign over them in mount Zion from henceforth, even forever.

And thou, O tower of the flock, the stronghold of the daughter of Zion, unto thee shall it come, even the first dominion; the kingdom shall come to the daughter of Jerusalem.

Above: The Ukrainian Orthodox Church in San Francisco, California, combines Byzantine and neo-Classical elements to present a dignified and heightened appearance that takes full advantage of its elevation above the street. The lower entrance is a parish hall, for wholesome activities not directly religious. Twin towers, pillars and dual entrance stairs give the impression that, at the upper doors, one is entering the abode of a king, as indeed one is.

THE CITY UPON THE HILL
—*Matthew 5:3 – 12 and 14 – 16*

In thy Kingdom remember us, oh Lord, when thou comest into thy Kingdom.

— *Orthodox chant*

Blessed are the poor in spirit: for theirs is the kingdom of heaven.

Blessed are they that mourn: for they shall be comforted.

Blessed are the meek: for they shall inherit the earth.

Blessed are they which do hunger and thirst after righteousness: for they shall be filled.

Blessed are the merciful: for they shall obtain mercy.

Blessed are the pure in heart: for they shall see God.

Blessed are the peacemakers: for they shall be called the children of God.

Blessed are they which are persecuted for righteousness' sake; for theirs is the kingdom of heaven.

Blessed are ye, when men shall revile you, and persecute you, and shall say all manner of evil against you falsely, for my sake.

Rejoice, and be exceeding glad: for great is your reward in heaven . . . .

Ye are the light of the world. A city that is set on a hill cannot be hid.

Neither do men light a candle, and put it under a bushel, but on a candlestick; and it giveth light unto all that are in the house.

Let your light so shine before men that they may see your good works, and glorify your Father which is in heaven.

Above: A view through the palms at the dome of this same church. This is a good architectural example of symbolic fulfillment — specifically, the dome represents the cosmos, a candle lit to heaven and the light of salvation bearing witness to all.

As can be seen here, it seems veritably a 'city on a hill.' Atop the burning light is the gleaming golden cross, creating yet another symbol — the cross on the orb, Christ's kingship over the world.

PSALM 136 and
PSALM 135:1–6, 9–14, 19–21

O give thanks unto the Lord; for he is good: for his mercy endureth forever.

O give thanks unto the God of gods: for his mercy endureth forever.

O give thanks to the Lord of lords: for his mercy endureth forever.

Praise ye the Lord. Praise ye the name of the Lord; praise him, O ye servants of the Lord.

Ye that stand in the house of the Lord, in the courts of the house of our God,

Praise the Lord, for the Lord is good: sing praises unto his name; for it is good.

For the Lord hath chosen Jacob unto himself, and Israel for his peculiar treasure.

For I know that the Lord is great, and that our Lord is above all gods.

. . . he maketh lightnings for the rain; he bringeth the wind out of his treasuries . . .

Who sent tokens and wonders into the midst of thee, O Egypt, upon Pharaoh, and upon all his servants.

Who smote great nations, and slew mighty kings;

Sihon king of the Amorites, and Og king of Bashan, and all the kingdoms of Cannaan:

And gave their land for a heritage, a heritage unto Israel his people.

Thy name, O Lord, endureth forever; and thy memorial, O Lord, throughout all generations.

For the Lord will judge his people, and he will repent himself concerning his servants.

Bless the Lord, O house of Israel: bless the Lord, O house of Aaron:

Bless the Lord, O house of Levi: yet that fear the Lord, bless the Lord.

Blessed be the Lord out of Zion, which dwelleth at Jerusalem. Praise ye the Lord.

These pages: A combination of Spanish and neo-Classical architecture presents a very beautiful composition of praise to God in the physical plant of the renovated Mission Santa Barbara, originally a spiritual way station on Father Junipero Serra's 'Royal Road.' The body of the church and the towers are distinctively Latin, and the entrance and steps are distinctly Greek, suggesting a missionary scope embracing East and West, Old World and New.

PLEASANT ARE THY COURTS

Pleasant are Thy courts above
In the land of light and love;
Pleasant are Thy courts below
In this land of sin and woe:
Oh, my spirit longs and faints
For the converse of Thy Saints,
For the brightness of Thy Face,
For Thy fullness, God of grace.

Happy birds that sing and fly
Round Thy Altars, O most High;
Happier souls that find redress
In a heavenly Father's rest;
Like the wandering dove that found
No repose on earth around,
They can to their ark repair,
And enjoy it ever there.

Happy souls, their praises flow
Even in this vale of woe;
Waters in the desert rise,
Manna feeds them from the skies;
On they go from strength to strength,
Till they reach Thy Throne at length,
At Thy feet adoring fall,
Who hast led them safe through all.

Lord, be mine this prize to win,
Guide me through a world of sin,
Keep me by Thy saving grace,
Give me at Thy side a place;
Sun and shield alike Thou art,
Guide and guard my erring heart;
Grace and glory flow from Thee;
Shower, O shower them, Lord, on me.

—Rev Francis H Lyte

At right: Old St Mary's Church of Nicasio Valley, California was established in 1867. The tower's triple eaves create an allusion to neo-Classic motifs, as they call attention to the roof-end behind it, which resembles a Greek pediment. White walls and a simple, gold Catholic cross lend an air of purity.

O GLADSOME LIGHT

O Gladsome Light
  of the Holy Glory
  of the Immortal Father
Heavenly, Holy,
  Blessed Jesus Christ.

Now that we have come
  to the setting of the sun,
  and behold the light of evening,
We praise God,
  Father, Son and Holy Spirit.

For meet it is
  at all times
To worship Thee
  with voices of praise,
Oh Son of God
  And Giver of Light —

Therefore all the world
Doth glorify Thee.

— *Orthodox Hymn*

At left: An unusual image of Mary, the Mother of God, at the beautiful Russian Orthodox Church of all the Saints, located in Burlingame, California. This image is slated to be redone in a more traditional iconographic form.

PSALM 134 and LUKE
1:30 – 35, 46 – 55

Behold, bless ye the Lord, all ye servants of the Lord, which by night stand in the house of the Lord.

Lift up your hand in the sanctuary, and bless the Lord.

The Lord that made heaven and earth bless thee out of Zion.

And the angel said unto her, Fear not, Mary: for thou hast found favor with God.

And behold, thou shalt conceive in thy womb, and bring forth a son, and shalt call his name Jesus.

He shall be great, and shall be called the Son of the Highest: and the Lord God shall give unto him the throne of his father David:

And he shall reign over the house of Jacob forever; and of his kingdom there shall be no end.

Then said Mary unto the angel, How shall this be, seeing I know not a man?

And the angel answered and said unto her, The Holy Ghost shall come upon thee, and the power of the Highest shall overshadow thee: therefore also that holy thing which shall be born of thee shall be called the Son of God . . . .

And Mary said, My soul doth magnify the Lord,

And my spirit hath rejoiced in God my Savior.

For he hath regarded the low estate of his handmaiden: for, behold, from henceforth all generations shall call me blessed.

For he that is mighty hath done to me great things, and holy is his name.

And his mercy is on them that fear him from generation to generation.

He hath shown strength with his arm; he hath scattered the proud in the imagination of their hearts.

He hath put down the mighty from their seats, and exalted them of low degree.

He hath filled the hungry with good things; and the rich he hath sent empty away.

He hath helped his servant Israel, in remembrance of his mercy;

As he spake to our fathers, to Abraham, and to his seed forever.

Above left: A closeup of three of the church's five domes (see caption on page 21) shows exceedingly fine gold leaf work and bas-relief stars. Note the filligree at the base of, and crosses atop, each dome (see caption, page 140). *Above:* A frontal view of the Russian Orthodox Church of All Saints. It is an octagon set into a cross, and thus embodies the oneness of belief, and the very center of belief symbolically. It is like a glimpse of another world.

ISAIAH 56:6 – 8 and PSALM 51:17 – 18

Also the sons of the stranger, that join themselves to the Lord, to serve him, and to love the name of the Lord, to be his servants, every one that keepth the sabbath from polluting it, and taketh hold of my covenant;

Even them will I bring to my holy mountain, and make them joyful in my house of prayer: their burnt offerings and their sacrifices shall be accepted upon mine altar; for mine house shall be called a house of prayer for all people.

The Lord God which gathereth the outcasts of Israel saith, Yet will I gather others to him, beside those that are gathered unto him.

The sacrifices of God are a broken spirit: a broken and a contrite heart, O God, thou wilt not despise.

Do good in thy good pleasure unto Zion: build thou the walls of Jerusalem.

At left: St Peter's Catholic Church at Kahaluu Bay, on the island of Hawaii was built on the site of an ancient temple. Compare this with the *above* church building, which is situated on the Hawaiian island of Molokai.

PSALM 91:1 – 9

He that dwelleth in the secret place of the most High shall abide under the shadow of the Almighty.

I will say of the Lord, He is my refuge and my fortress: my God; in him will I trust.

Surely he shall deliver thee from the snare of the fowler, and from the noisome pestilence.

He shall cover thee with his feathers, and under his wings shalt thou trust: his truth shall be thy shield and buckler.

Thou shalt not be afraid for the terror by night; nor for the arrow that flieth by day;

Nor for the pestilence that walketh in darkness; nor for the destruction that wasteth at noonday.

A thousand shall fall at thy side, and ten thousand at thy right hand; but it shall not come nigh thee.

Only with thine eyes shalt thou behold and see the reward of the wicked.

Because thou has made the Lord, which is my refuge, even the most High, thy habitation.

Above: Save for its extremely weather-beaten appearance and its exotic surroundings, this ancient-looking (but not really all that old) church at Keomuku, on the Hawaiian island of Lanai, is similar to many country churches elsewhere in North America. *At right:* A steeple challenges the dense matter of this world, in a Hawaiian photograph that is architecturally instructive. Whether in Hawaii or a locale such as Pennsylvania, the typical country church of frame construction changes little.

from

PRAYER

'Our Father.'

The mother's voice was low and tender, and solemn.

'Our Father.'

On two small voices the tones were borne upward.

'Who are in heaven.'

'Who are in heaven,' repeated the children.

'Hallowed be thy name.'

Lower fell the voices of the little ones. In a gentle murmur they said,

'Hallowed be thy name.'

'Thy kingdom come.'

And the burden of prayer was still taken by the children —

'Thy will be done on earth as it is in heaven,' filled the chamber.

And the mother continued,

'Give us this day our daily bread.'

'Our daily bread,' lingered a moment on the air, as the mother's voice was hushed into silence.

'And forgive us our debts as we also forgive our debtors. And lead us not into temptation, but deliver us from evil. For thine is the kingdom, and the power, and the glory, forever. Amen.'

All these holy words were said piously and fervently by the little ones, as they knelt with clasped hands beside their mother. Then their thoughts, uplifted on the wings of prayer to their heavenly Father, came back again and rested on their earthly parents.

Then, as their heads rested side by side on the pillows, the mother's last goodnight kiss was given, and the shadowy curtains drawn.

A stillness reigns without the chamber. Inwardly, the parents' ears are bent. They have given those innocent ones into the keeping of God's angels, and they can almost hear the rustle of their garments as they gather around the sleeping babes. A sigh, deep and tremulous, breaks on the air. Quickly the mother turns to the father of her children, with a look of earnest inquiry upon her countenance. And he answers thus her silent questions:

'Far back through many years have my thoughts been wandering. At my mother's knee, thus I said my nightly childhood's evening prayer. It was that best and holiest of all prayers, ''Our Father,'' that she taught me.

'Childhood and my mother passed away. I went forth as a man into the world — strong, confident and self-seeking. Once I came into great temptation. Had I fallen in that temptation, I should have fallen never to rise again.

'I was about yielding. All the barriers I could oppose to it seemed just ready to give way, when — as I sat in my room one evening — there came from an adjoining chamber, the

continued on page 190

At right: St Sophia Catholic Church, 'Our Lady of Sorrows,' at Kaluaaha, on Molokai. This locale enforces a simple, light construction, due to weathering and the small congregations of rural Hawaii. The longhouse-style church at Mauna Loa Plantation Settlement, *above,* is also found on Molokai.

continued from page 188

murmur of low voices. I listened. At first no articulate sound was heard, and yet something in the tones stirred my heart with new and strong emotions. At length there came to my ears, in the earnest, loving voice of a woman, the words, ''Deliver us from evil.''

'For an instant, it seemed to me as if that voice were that of my mother. Back with a sudden bound — through all the intervening years — went my thoughts, and I was again a child kneeling at my mother's knee. Humbly and reverently I said over the words of the holy prayer she had taught me, heart and eye uplifted to heaven. The power of darkness had passed. I was no longer standing in slippery places, with a flood of water ready to sweep me to destruction; but my feet were on a rock.

'In the holy words my mother had taught me in childhood was a living power to resist evil through all my life. That unknown mother — as she taught her child to repeat this evening prayer — how little dreamed she that the holy words were to reach a stranger's ears, and save him through the memory of his own childhood and his own mother. What a power there is in God's word, as it flows into and rests in the minds of innocent childhood.'

Tears were in the eyes of the wife and mother, as she lifted her face and gazed with tenderness upon the countenance of her husband. Her heart was too full for utterance. A little while she thus gazed, and then laid her hand upon his bosom. Angels were in the chamber where their dear ones slept, and they felt their holy presence.

— *MA Vroman*

At right and above: Views of the (Swedenborgian) Wayfarers Chapel in Rancho Palos Verdes, California — designed by Frank Lloyd Wright; built in 1951. *Overleaf:* West Point's Cadet Chapel — what wars are waged within its walls?